My Life's Journey from Ukraine to Maine

As told by Dr. Maria Myroslava Tanczak-Dycio
to Martha Stevens-David

To Judy
from
Mary T. Dycio
aug 20/17

PRGott Publishing
P.O. Box 43, Norway, Maine 04268
www.prgottbooks.net

Cover and interior images are the property of Dr. Dycio.
Front cover painting of Ukrainian cottage is by Dr. Dycio.
Layout by Laura Ashton, laura@gitflorida.com

Copyright © 2013 by Dr. Maria Myroslava Tanczak-Dycio

First Printing

ISBN: 978-1492878612

Printed in the United States of America

PRGott Books Publishing

Author Foreword

The reason that I wanted to write my biography is because I never thought I would; after all, I'm not the only one who has an interesting story to tell. But my children, my friends and my relatives all said, "Oh Mary, just do it! You know, you are getting old and there aren't many left in the world like you, and very few people in their old age have had such a good memory, an interesting life or want to write their biography."

So, that is why I postponed it year after year, and then my best friend, Dr. Hector Arrache, when I mentioned it to him, said that he knows a lady who will help me because: "Your English is very good but not that good. She will help you to write your biography. She will help you. Why don't you do it?"

I recently celebrated my ninety-first birthday, and I don't know if I will live another nine years to celebrate my hundredth birthday. So I figured to myself, *What do I have to lose? Let's do it!* If it turns out well, that's good. I hope that it will be a best seller and maybe they will take my story to Hollywood!

I still speak English with a slight Ukrainian accent, and the flavor of my accent and choice of words here in my memoir will show this. I hope you like my story.

Dr. Maria Myroslava "Gloria" Tanczak -Dycio

My Life's Journey from Ukraine to Maine

As told by Dr. Maria Myroslava Tanczak-Dycio
to Martha Stevens-David

Embroidery by Dr. Dycio in a typical Ukraine design

Ukraine

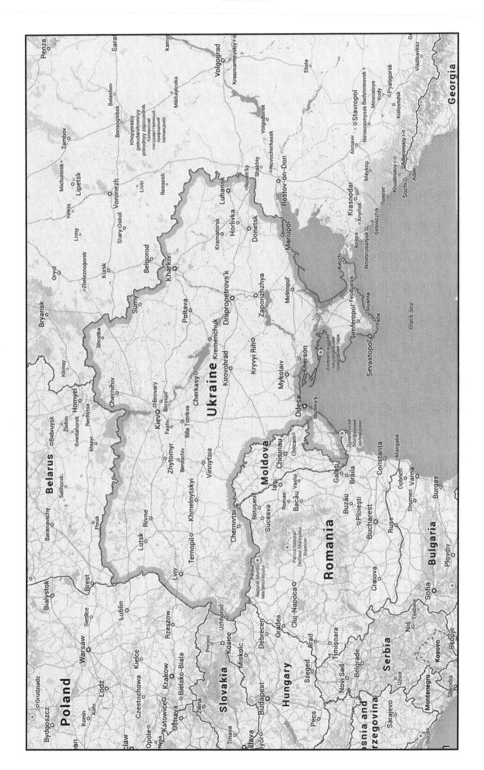

My Life's Story:

I was born July tenth, nineteen twenty-two in Rybnyky, West Ukraine, a place where my father, a priest, had his parish. But for some reason they made a mistake and they wrote on my birth certificate—July eleventh—which made me one day younger. I don't know if it was the priest who wrote it down wrong or the school, but I really don't mind.

Although I was born in Ukraine, at that time it was really West Ukraine and belonged to Poland. I was born into the family of a Ukrainian Catholic Priest. In the Western world, that would be considered very unusual. People think that I must be Orthodox but I explained to them that I am not Orthodox. My father was a Ukrainian Catholic priest. In the Roman Catholic Church, there are about five different rites which all belong to Rome and all belong to the pope. They have different rites but the same beliefs.

Our priests are different from the Roman Catholic priests because they can get married, but it must be before they are ordained. If a priest's wife dies after they are ordained, then they have to be celibate. Then they cannot marry.

My parents married when they were young. My mother was just twenty and my father was only twenty-six when I was born. My mother was a school teacher. My real name is not Mary. My name is Maria Myroslava "Gloria" Tanczak. At home they called me Marusia.

I had a very happy childhood. My parents, especially my father, were wonderful to me. My mother was stricter but she was not too bad, and I had a wonderful, wonderful grandma. She was my mother's mother and a big boss of all of us and she decided what was done in my family. She was called *Baba* in my country and she lived with us. On my mother's side, most of the men were priests and this goes back many centuries. On my father's side, they were all mostly farmers.

In the village where my father held his first position as a priest, he was very happy because it was very close to his birth place and he could visit his parents who were still alive. And the city, Berezhany, was only about five miles from his birthplace and where he attended high school. And another thing that made my parents very happy about living in that beautiful place is that there was a train station just within walking distance and my mother could go shopping anytime she wanted, even if she didn't have any money. My mother loved to shop.

Due to all the fighting during the First World War, when my father moved to the new parish, he had no place to live because all the parish houses, stables, and barns had been destroyed during the war between the Austrians, Russians, and later the Ukrainian and Polish soldiers. My father built a stable for the animals and renovated the church. Then he built a parish house and we lived there. I remember a corridor, a small guest room, a big kitchen, a dining room, a little room for my grandma, a small bathroom and a beautiful living room where we children were not allowed to go. That living room had to be spotless because my mother was crazy about having a clean house, and this living room was for guests only. Probably it was not really beautiful to others, but to me it was beautiful.

When I was about three years old, somebody introduced me to a new little cry-baby who had come to our house, and I was not happy about him at all. Then they told me that the little cry-baby was my new little brother, Myron. Everybody was running around and playing with him and ignoring me like I was nothing, and I became very jealous and I didn't like it. I never played with him, I only tolerated him.

My brother was now the pampered one, and I hated that. I was now about five years old and he was about two, and everyone would go to him and say, "Oh such a cute baby!" "Oh, what a sweet baby!" "Oh, what a beautiful little boy!" Everyone who came to our home always praised my brother and I was always left out. It seemed to me that everyone couldn't see me and I thought that I must be very homely looking. I thought that I was not pretty because I had carrot colored hair and many freckles and I was jealous of all the attention that he was getting from all the family. So one day my jealously overwhelmed me and I bit him on the hand. His little hand became infected and started to swell all up and they had to take him to the doctor. Oh boy, did I get hell from my mother, and my father was very upset with me, too. I couldn't understand why they were so upset. As a small child I was always very jealous of Myron.

We had plenty of nannies and maids because that's how it was in Ukraine because there was no electricity or machines to do the work. My mother was very lady-like and she didn't have to work outside our home like other mothers did.

My nanny really wasn't very well-educated, she was only a village girl, but she was very nice. Every once in a while, she wanted me to play with my little brother but I just didn't want to. Somehow, I just couldn't stand the thought that he received more attention than I did.

My father had a good friend, a professor who was an alumnus of the academy—we called it a "gymnasium"—in Berezhany. One day he visited that friend and told him that he was now the proud father of a beautiful baby girl— me. That professor had a whole bunch of puppies, and come to find out those puppies were born on the same day as me. The professor gave my father a beautiful little puppy and would you believe it, that dog was my best friend until I turned fifteen years of age when she died. I slept with her, I dressed her up, I fed her, and that dog allowed me to do whatever I wanted to do with her. She was my beautiful, constant companion and when I went off to school, I would visit her every chance I got. That dog loved me as much as any dog can love a human being. And to tell you the truth, I still love her till this day. Her name was Mushka, which means "small fly."

Even though I had a happy childhood, I did have a horrible enemy. My mother had poultry which she used to sell to make some money for the family during the holidays. In that flock she had a huge monster goose that was bigger than me. I hated him and he hated me and we started a big war! He would run after me and I would run so fast that he couldn't get me, but one day somebody was smart and gave me a big stick. Then I felt that I was safe so I would go and hit him with the stick; but one day he was smarter than me and he bit me something horrible on the buttocks. I remember that I screamed and hollered and everybody came to my rescue. After that, I never saw that goose again; I think we ate him for supper.

I remember that that parish had a gorgeous orchard because in Ukraine the earth was very fertile. Those orchards were full of fruit trees such as cherries, apples, plums and pears. I remember the beautiful cherries because in the summer my father would sell the cherries. Some men would come to pick them up to sell them to the local stores. I loved to go to the orchard, but my mother would not allow me to go there because it was such a huge place and she was afraid for me. But if the nanny was going there with my brother, then we could go to the orchard and see the fruit and sometimes we would take some sandwiches and have a lovely picnic.

Our home was full of guests every summer and for every holiday and most especially on Christmas. Our home was always so happy and everyone seemed to be happy too. They were all very young. My father came from a family of four children, and he was the oldest. His youngest brother, who was fourteen years younger than my father, was really raised in our home. His siblings used to come every summer, and my mother's youngest brother, who was also studying to be a priest, would also come to stay every summer with us. Because my grandmother didn't have a place to go to, she stayed with us too.

My mother's brother, who was fourteen years older than her, was a professor. He studied in Vienna in German studies and he was very bright. He went to Stryj and they appointed him superintendent of a woman's seminary school. He had two children: a girl ten years older than me, and a boy who was two years older than me. His wife, my aunt, was very quiet and a very nice lady.

In the early years, I couldn't stand my cousins; they hated me and I hated their guts too. Because I was the youngest, they liked to push me around, but later on as we grew older, we all became good friends. The girl went on to become a lawyer. As I told you before, my childhood was wonderful and I think we stayed in that first parish six or seven years.

My father was an exceptionally talented businessman and a farmer. He was a very bright man and so smart. After World War One, he went to college for two years because he wanted to become a professor; but my grandfather, his father, told him that the Poles do not want the Ukrainians to get a good job and they persecuted the Ukrainians. He told my father to go and study theology and become a priest. In that time, the priests were all farmers because that was the only way you could support yourself unless you lived in a city.

So he did as his father asked, and six years later he became a priest. He worked very hard to make repairs to the church in that parish. One day, the dean came to visit him and told my father that he was interested in that parish for himself. You know, you have nothing to say when you are just a priest. You must do as you are told. My father was very upset but there was nothing that he could do. We served the dean only the very best food during his visit, and after he had left, my father was not a happy man after that. He was very worried that we were going to be thrown out and he would be sent to another parish.

My grandmother had nine children, and she later told me that in those days the children were dying from all kinds of diseases. The children were vaccinated for smallpox and that was all, but not for scarlet fever, whooping cough and measles. You name it and we had it in Ukraine. Of my grandmother's nine beautiful children, four contracted deadly illnesses and they died. It was common knowledge that anyone who had at least five children, maybe two of them will die from some childhood illness. The ones that remained were her five youngest children.

My mother was the youngest. Next to her was a sister Maria, who was two years older, and then a brother, Zenon, who became a priest, and Omelan, the oldest, was a professor. One of the boys, who was thought to be a genius, was studying engineering and when World War One broke out between the Austrian Empire and the Russians, he was called away to fight. He went and was fighting on the Italian front, and sadly at age twenty-two, he was killed.

My mother's oldest brother, who was fourteen years older than she, was a part-time professor of the German language and the Ukrainian language. And the last two years of his studies, he studied in Vienna. At that time, to have the chance to study in Vienna was something out of this world and it was thought to be very "stylish" if the students could go to finish their studies in Vienna. He had just completed his studies when World War One started.

My mother's sister, Maria, was a lovely looking lady and an excellent pianist and also a teacher. In those days usually all the women became teachers. She was engaged to a student who was in law school and he was born into a priest's family who lived next door. Then the war started and he, too, went off to war. As was the custom back then, my grandmother had prepared everything for her daughter's *trousseau* and her wedding, and fortunately for her, she never married him.

In the meantime, it was nineteen-eighteen, war started and Emperor Franz Joseph died, and Austria lost the war. Then the Poles and Ukrainians started to fight for their independence. The Ukrainians finally achieved their independence but that only lasted about four years because we lost our independence to the Communists and the Poles.

My mother's father was about sixty-five or sixty-six years old in nineteen-eighteen and in his village there was an epidemic of typhus. The typhus infection came from a lice infestation. He was a priest and a dean and he was a very smart man who had finished his theology studies in Vienna. He went to give the last rites to a very sick farmer and apparently he was bitten by lice because my grandmother found the lice on his shirt; he contracted typhus and he died.

When he died the misery started. We were still at war and there was a law that if a priest dies, then the priest's wife has to leave the parish because another priest will come to fill that vacancy. In that time, they used to give the priest's wife a small pension. My aunt who was engaged when the war started—well, her husband-to-be, he left her. When my grandfather died, they went from well-to-do into poverty and the Hungarian and Polish soldiers came and stole everything she had. And they wounded her. After she recovered, my grandmother had to leave the parish house and she moved to a small farmer's house in the village.

In the meantime, the Poles came back and became independent, and our West Ukraine lost its independence and it became a part of Poland. My aunt had no job because she did not want to teach in Poland, so she became a private teacher for my parents' friends' children. She had about four or five students and she would teach them at home because it would be cheaper for everyone.

By now my aunt was getting old and she had nobody to marry. She was teaching all the time and my father always tried to find ways to help everybody. He had a friend who was very smart and he lived quite a distance from us. This friend had studied theology and he was not yet a priest. At that time, you could only marry before you had taken your final vows as a priest and if you were married and your wife died, you could not remarry. You can only marry once in your life and you also could not get a divorce.

So my father arranged a meeting between his friend and my aunt, and of course, my aunt had not married after her fiancé left her. She was still heartbroken because she had loved that young man. Well, she did marry my father's friend.

They had two children. The girl was a very beautiful singer, and the boy, well, he was much younger than me and I think that he finished in the engineering school. In that marriage my aunt was always sickly. My father and mother later told me that at the young age of forty-two, she died from tuberculosis. It is so sad to think how miserable some people's lives were.

In the meantime, my mother, who was very beautiful and some even thought she was gorgeous because she was very small with very dark, brunette hair. My mother had met my father when she went to visit her uncle. My father was very handsome and she was beautiful. They fell in love and they were a very loveable couple. They adored each other and he spoiled her rotten. She loved to dress up and if a fork was dropped on the floor, she didn't have to pick it up if she didn't want to.

She was very lucky because my grandmother Ewanna-Joanna Levensky-Cisyk was a genius, a very good housekeeper, an excellent cook, and an excellent gardener. She excelled in everything she did; she was a very smart woman. In those days, girls only had to go to school for seven grades. They were taught A-Class French, then German because we were now under German occupation, then Polish. They were taught how to play the piano, how to cook, how to sew. They taught the girls how to be a good housewife because at that time, the girls usually got married at the age of seventeen. Most married priests or lawyers but if they were lucky, some even married doctors, though at that time there were very few doctors.

My father always said that during the Austrian occupation, Ukrainians had a good life. We did try to become independent from the Austrians, but at that time, Franz Joseph, who was the Austrian Emperor, was supposed to be a very "humane" emperor. If you had a good education and you really wanted to, you could always get a good job in the post office or with the state or a secretary in city hall. At that time, there were no telephones.

My grandmother's siblings were three boys and two girls. The oldest girl was married to a priest at age sixteen, and her youngest sister, who was supposed to be very smart, took a state exam and became a teacher. She met a priest who taught in a local school. She married him and she had a very, very good life. They only had one child, who died at the age of seven from scarlet fever. She never had other children and she never had to work because her husband had enough income, so they traveled to Rome, Vienna and Germany. You know, that was before World War One.

My grandmother's sister had a very nice apartment in Lviv, and this was during the Austrian occupation. She always had maids and she used to visit us once in a while. My mother used to say, "Oh no! She's coming!" And "Now I have to wash, I have to clean, or she is going to notice everything!" And my mother was right because my grandaunt always used to find something wrong with everything.

After my grandfather died, my grandmother moved out of the parish house that she had shared with my grandfather and moved into a small farm house in the village. And right after my parents got married, she immediately packed her things and she moved into the parish house with us. As I remember, in that home, nobody was boss but my grandmother. If my mother, or God forbid my father, tried to tell her how to do something, she'd say, "What do you know?" "That's not the right way!" "I want to do this." "I want to do that!" She was always the boss and they had plenty of maids to help in whatever way she wanted and my parents always obeyed her.

Because our new parish house was situated on a large farm,

the workers would come to work at six o'clock in the morning. My grandmother was already up waiting for them and she would tell them what to do. Sometimes my father didn't like her being the boss, but there was nothing he could do about it. My mother too, didn't like it but she would always ask, "Ma, what do you think?" "Ma, what do you say?" All the farm workers and the village people respected my grandmother.

Besides running our family's life and the farm life, my grandmother was always playing the role of a nurse. She was not a trained nurse, but whenever anybody in the village had an illness or injury, she would always go to help them.

Every so often, she would make all kinds of medication. She had a large closet where she kept all of her medical supplies locked up. She would go out into our beautiful gardens and gather herbs and leaves from the plants or flowers and make her own medicines. She would take the petals from the white lily leaves and put them in alcohol and let them soak for a while. And these old home remedies really worked!

She had a special secret way of making gin. Since we had juniper plants, she would have the workers bring her the juniper berries and she and my mother could make gin better than they made in the factories. I don't remember how old I was, but once they gave me some of that gin because I had a cough, and once I tasted that mixture, I wanted more. I loved that taste! I would go to my grandmother, not my mother, and I would say to her, "Grandma, give me gin." Oh, I was very smart; I knew how to handle them all. I knew how to get what I wanted. I would hold my belly and double over as though I was in severe pain and cry, "Oh, my stomach. It hurts so bad!"

My grandmother would rush over to my side and say, "What's the matter baby?" If I had gone to my mother, she would look at me and say, "Go lie down and I will give you tea."

I would run to my grandmother and cry and say, "Grandmother, I am dying from this horrible pain! Can't you help me?"

She would push my arms away and touch my belly. "You are not dying. Your belly is nice and soft." She would raise her eyes to mine and say, "I will give you some gin." After drinking what she had given me, I still wanted more, I would cry some more and say that my stomach still hurt. I may have only been six years old but I was very smart and I knew how to outsmart most of the adults in my family!

I couldn't fool my mother though. If my grandmother was not around I would go to my mother and if she scolded me, I would make believe that I was crying. If my father heard me, he would rush to my defense. "Hey, what are you doing to that poor baby? Why do you make her cry?" My grandmother and my father always called me "poor baby", but not my mother. My mother could always see through me and I didn't like that. I won't say that I didn't like her but she was very strict with me. But my father and my grandmother were blinded by their love. Of all her grandchildren, it seemed that my grandmother liked me and my baby brother the best.

By this time I was about six years old, and it was time for me to attend school and I didn't like it at all. I hated the school from the very beginning. My mother was a teacher and when she saw how I hated that school, she decided that she would teach me herself at home. This was one of the worst times in my life! I couldn't play anymore; I had to sit still and study the alphabet and I had to learn to read and write and I couldn't do the math. Try as she might, I never could learn one and one and two and two. I struggled and struggled and finally finished the first year. After that my mother decided that she couldn't teach me anything and she told me that she was going to send me back to the regular school because I was horrible at studying.

My father's brother who lived with us most of the time, except when he was going to school, was also a very gifted man. He could play many musical instruments very well, especially the guitar, and he decided that he would teach me music. This was the second worst time of my life. I couldn't play outside anymore, which I loved. Now I had to study, study, study all the time.

I had two friends, one of whom was my grandmother, and whenever I did anything wrong, I would run to my Grammy and make believe that I was crying and whine and carry on, and my father was my other best friend. I always thought that my mother loved my brother more than me. I always thought that, but in later years, after thinking about it, maybe I was wrong because later when we were grown, she was very good to me.

Not too long after that, my father received the bad news that the dean wanted that parish and we would have to pack up and move out. I remember that we had to move to a northern village. In those days, there were no cars, no electricity, no nothing. We had to hook the horses to the carriages, and I loved it because there was so much excitement. My parents were busy putting everything in boxes and packing all the household goods in the wagons. We had to put everything in big carts and hook them to the horses. The other farm animals were tied to the back of the carts or put into the carts and we had about ten or fifteen wagons filled with my mother's furniture and animals.

The morning that we moved, there was my father and my mother, my grandmother, two nannies and the maids, and we moved to Sernyky, a place that was over a hundred miles away. It took us about two full days to get to that village. My father didn't like that village because it was very far away from all civilization and there were no buses or trains and it didn't even have a high school or a middle school. There was nothing there. The closest small town was about fifty miles away.

My father disliked that village, but the parish house was very beautiful. It was quite new and it had beautiful gardens and orchards. Ukrainians always had beautiful orchards. The priest who lived there had died and my father took his place. The house had a large kitchen and plenty of rooms. There was a room for my grandmother and my parent's bedroom, a living room, a dining room, a guest room and beautiful verandas. It was a gorgeous home for a priest. The old priest had been living there for more than thirty years and he had large stables for all the animals. The church was also made of wood and very beautiful.

For me, that isolated village was paradise. I loved it there and I became like a little tree monkey. I became so good that I could jump or swing from tree to tree and I loved it! I didn't have any friends to play with because they all lived far away from the parish. Finally, I found myself a little girlfriend when a young woman, whose husband had died, came to work at our house and she brought her little girl with her. We always had many workers to care for the huge orchards, fields and animals, and there was a lovely girl who shepherded the geese and fowl.

By this time, I was in the second grade and at first I was very bashful but then I found out that I was *persona grata*, a very important

17

person, because I was the priest's daughter. It didn't take me long to figure that out. Everyone had to be very nice to me and I thought that I didn't have to study. The school had a husband and wife and they were my teachers. This young couple became very good friends of my parents, and I figured that if my parents and my teachers were such good friends, then I didn't need to study. If they were my friends, then they should just give me an "A".

I hated school and studying and I hated books too! After school I would run away to the orchards with my friend and we would climb the apple trees and throw apples at each other and have lots of fun, fun, fun. We had six dogs and many, many cats, and I loved our dogs but I didn't care for the cats! But then, the cats didn't come into our house; they usually lived in the barns with the other animals where they always had plenty of things to eat. My mother was the one who loved the cats, and she always had one or two in the house with her. What a beautiful place that was for me!

I stayed in my grandmother's room with my brother. She had a big bed and we loved it. By now, I was seven or eight years old and I was becoming more civilized. I didn't bother my brother as much, and now he was going to school too. One day I heard my father and a few other priests saying that if you want to have a good job anywhere, then you have to change to a be a Roman Catholic.

Then we heard that the Poles were arresting a lot of Ukrainian people. But our Ukrainian people outsmarted the Poles. They started to organize a kind of democracy for themselves. They opened all kinds of private stores and huge slaughter houses. They would take the pigs and slaughter them and send the meat away to be sold. My father had about two dozen cows and he would send the milk to the village to the private Ukrainian milk house where it would be made into butter. Ukrainians started all kinds of businesses without the Poles and they started to make money and they created all kinds of jobs, and the Poles were not happy with us.

One day when I was in the third or fourth grade, we got a new history book, and on the front cover there was a picture of the Mr. Joseph Pilsucky, the President of the Polish state. I looked at that big picture and I remembered hearing my father always saying something about the

Poles. I decided that I would make myself very smart. Guess what I did? I drew on the cover of the history book on the Polish President's picture! I drew him with big horns and a long tail just like the Devil. I took my book with the altered cover and showed it to all the other students. The teacher, a woman, asked me, "Marusia, what do you have?" So, I went and showed her. I said, "Look what I have done!" The teacher took my book with my drawing on the cover and I never saw that book again! And that day after school, I went home and guess what? Both of my teachers had come to visit my parents.

They told my father how smart I am and then they showed my father my drawing on the picture of the Polish President. And boy did I get holy hell! My father said to me, "Do you want those teachers to lose their jobs? What came over you? What do you have against the Poles?" After that, my father was very careful about what he said in front of me because he didn't want me to get things in my head. Anyway, I promised all of them that I would never draw anything like that again.

I was never a scholar. I still didn't like school and I hated to study. I was happiest when I was out of school and playing in the woods. I loved the woods and the flowers. I was a nature girl, not a scholar.

Then came fourth grade, my last grade in that small school house. So my mother and my grandmother started to prepare me by telling me that I must go to my uncle's school. He had a grammar school where the children went for seven years, and this school was for both boys and girls. And he also was in charge of a middle school. If you wanted to be a doctor or a lawyer, you had to go to a school they called a "gymnasium." This was a very advanced school and you must study very hard.

There was also a seminary where they taught only girls to be teachers. That scared me a little because I had never wanted to go to school. I thought that four years was plenty for me. I didn't know that I had to go to school again. I was very unhappy and I hated my aunt and uncle's two kids. The girl was older than me and she was very bossy and she had already nearly finished in the gymnasium. She was very smart but I still didn't like her.

By now I was ten years old, and my mother began packing my things to get me ready to go and live at my uncle's. That didn't make me very happy because at that time, school started on the third of September.

At about August twentieth, I was all packed and I was supposed to go with my uncle, aunt and their two kids to live with them in Stryj. I hated the idea. At the end of August, the weather was already turning cold and I thought that I was very smart and I had to do something so that I wouldn't have to go to live with them. So I decided to stay outside in the cold fall air and catch a cold. I thought that maybe they will be scared that I am sick and they will leave me alone and I won't have to go to that horrible place with those horrible people. I remember that I was coughing and sneezing, but that didn't help me at all. My grandmother, who always nursed the villagers, gave me some of her home made medicine, packed me up, and I went to live in Stryj.

My aunt and uncle were wonderful to me, I can say that. They had a nice apartment; in those days most people didn't have a house. I had to stay in a room with my older cousin and my misery started. Of course I was quite behind in school because I didn't want to study. I couldn't understand anything. At night, my uncle tried to teach me math and the Polish language. If my older, smarter cousin tried to teach me too, she would always scream and holler at me, and believe me, that was the worst part of my life, and believe me, the schooling part of it was hell too! By now, at the school, I was no longer the "Priest's daughter," I was just a "regular" kid; I was just treated like nothing. That was hell!

But my aunt and uncle treated me very well. They had a beautiful apartment with a maid. There was a bunch of boys who lived in that area who used to play football, and since they didn't have enough boys to play the game, they invited me into their game and they always threw the ball at me. Of course I was very poor at that game, and everybody hit me with the ball. They screamed and hollered at me calling me an idiot, a retard, etc., etc. They were two or three years older than me and I came home with all kinds of injuries, broken nails, skinned fingers, scratches and bruises, and my cousin told me that if I showed my injuries to my aunt or uncle they would punish me so horribly that they might even kill me! It was not true, but that horrible cousin did scare me. When I was eating I held my hands and fingers so that my aunt and uncle could not see my injuries.

I hated it there and I used to cry every night when going to bed and every morning when I got up at six o'clock and again when I'd have to go to school. But, like everything else, that year passed and I finally found four very nice girlfriends. They invited me to their homes and I started to get used to that place, but I was still a poor student. I went there for three years and then they changed all the schooling in Poland and I had to go to a gymnasium.

By now it was nineteen thirty-five, and my uncle lost his job. The Poles were really pushing the Ukrainians. They put young students in jail because they figured that all Ukrainians are German spies. This was the time that Hitler had come into power, and he promised every nation who was under the yoke that they would be freed. Why those politicians couldn't see through all this, I never understood. But anyway, the Poles continued to treat Ukrainians very harshly.

In the meantime, my uncle's smart daughter had finished her second year of law school and she was arrested with a bunch of other students. She didn't have to stay in the prison very long, and after several months, she returned home. She had a boyfriend who was also a law student, and I'm sure that at that time, they were in Ukrainian underground. At that time, many Ukrainians belonged to Ukrainian underground, an organization to fight for our independence.

When she came home, she was thrown out of law school and I was still in Stryj, in school. One of my cousins was a professor in a gymnasium in Lublin which was a Catholic school and connected to the pope in Rome and the Catholic university. That uncle and aunt helped her to apply to the Catholic University in Lublin, and they accepted her. The university didn't care that she had been in jail, they accepted her, and she was very lucky because she was able to finish her law school studies there.

In the meanwhile, my poor uncle lost his job, that good job he had, mainly because his daughter had been arrested. He became a "regular" gymnasium teacher and a Professor of German Languages, at which he was excellent. But his pay was not as good as before.

Then my aunt started getting sick. She had so many worries. She was worried about her daughter all the time and she had some kidney infections and kidney problems. They were still living in their beautiful apartment, but because of her medical expenses, they decided to move to a smaller apartment because it would be cheaper.

I had finished my second year with them and now I had to go to the gymnasium. I had to take a very tough entrance exam. I'm not ashamed to say it again—I was not a good student. If it wasn't for my uncle, I would not have made it into this advanced school. My uncle helped me so much.

My aunt kept saying to me, "Marusia, don't worry, I will teach you German and you will be okay." I actually knew more German language than Polish, and somehow a miracle happened and I passed the entrance exam. I really don't know how because the math teacher, who was a friend of my uncle, told him that I had no idea what two and two were. And even though my uncle had taught me, I really was "unteachable"! I remember that professor who was in charge of the entrance exam. He took his head in his hands and said, "Oh my God! You know nothing about mathematics!" And I really couldn't speak Polish all that well either. You know, when I was younger and living in that little Ukrainian village, the teacher didn't try to teach me Polish, so how could I understand that language now? So now I entered the gymnasium.

In the meantime it was not so bad. My younger brother was becoming a little more civilized and we began to better understand each other. At the gymnasium it was very tough and we still had to study four languages. I still had my four or five girlfriends and my aunt was very happy that I had made friends with them because they were all from good homes.

I had become very friendly with a lawyer's daughter. Her father was an excellent lawyer in a large law firm. I couldn't understand, because to me, he was very old, although his wife must have only been in her late forties. They had five sons and my friend was their last child and their only daughter. And those sons were already grown, with the youngest son around twenty and she was only ten. Somehow she was so pampered. Her nanny would even take her to school and back.

My aunt used to give me a simple lunch with bread and butter and sometimes she'd put an egg in between. Once in a great while, she'd give me a baloney sandwich and sometimes my father sent me apples or plums. But my friend had oranges and chocolate for lunch. And my mother would tell me that I wasn't supposed to eat too much chocolate because I would have bad teeth. But if something special happened and we were able to get some chocolate, my mother would only give me a small piece to eat and then the next day she'd give me another little piece.

My grandmother loved Christmas and she'd decorate everything that she could and our home was always very beautiful, especially during the holidays. Two or three weeks before Christmas, my grandmother would make all kinds of candies. In those days, everything was homemade. She'd make some chocolate candies, some candy with nuts, and some marshmallow candy. She'd buy beautiful paper of gold and red to wrap the candies and fudge in. My mother would pick walnuts for us to eat. My father had a special tree of small Paradise apples. We only had a few of those trees and the apples were very small and oh, how we loved those little apples and all would go to the Christmas tree.

Since our ceilings were so high in that room, we used to have a very tall Christmas tree. When I grew older, I used to help them decorate that tree. We had many decorations because I had a cousin Doris who was very good at making them. My mother used to string popcorn on the tree with garlands and flowers. It was always very beautiful.

I never liked dolls and whatever dolls I was given, I didn't like them; but one year I got a dollhouse and it was really beautiful. We only got oranges at Christmas because they were the cheapest at that time. My mother would take an orange and five of us would be sitting at the table. She would peel the orange and then she would take a section and give it to my father, then my grandmother would give some to us kids, and I was lucky because my father always gave his share to me. That was the only time I got to eat oranges, and sometimes St. Nicholas would bring us Mandarin oranges as a special treat. My mother knew how I loved art and she always bought me crayons and lots of papers for me to draw on.

We always celebrated Christmas on Christmas Eve. The food had to be very special. There were always twelve dishes, all with no meat. On Christmas morning at six o'clock we would go to church. This holiday was usually a three-day celebration and all the villages would have carolers. Normally, we didn't receive presents but on our "name" day, I always received gifts. Gifts like books or a scarf or mittens. My gifts were always something very practical. Children received their gift not on Christmas night but on St. Nicholas' night of December sixth.

When I was three years old, I remember that one of our maids was cleaning peas and I wanted to help her. So she showed me how to open the pea shell and clean the peas. I took one of the little round green peas and I put it in my nose. And I looked at the maid and said, "Gogo," which means "peas" in a child's language. But nobody paid any attention to me. The next day, when I was crying and trying to tell them what I had done, the maid told my mother that I might have put a pea in my nose. Well, everybody paid attention to me then! My grandmother put some salve up my nose and my nose started to turn red and swell up. They tried all of my grandmother's secret recipes but nothing helped. And then my father said that he had better take me to the doctor. When it came to those types of things, my father was always in charge, not my mother.

It was a cloudy day and my father took me to Berezhany and I loved it! I remember that doctor was a good friend of my parents. Before we went to his office, my father took me to a toy store and he bought me some kind of toy and I remember that as we were leaving the store, the sun came out. My father looked at the bright sun and said, "Marusia, look! Look at the bright sun!"

I remember that I looked up into the bright sunshine and I had a terrific urge to sneeze . . . then that little green pea came flying out of my nose! My father bent down and picked it up and then he said to me, "Marusia, look at the pea!" When I looked at that little green pea, I could see that it had already begun to send out roots! The pea had already begun to grow in my nose! But looking back, I realize that I was so mean when I was a child that even God didn't want me. And even the Devil didn't want me. Nobody wanted me! My father was so happy that the pea had come out because he was very afraid that I would have to have surgery. He took me back to the toy store and bought me another little toy. That was the only time in my life that I got two toys in one day.

Now, I was still living in Stryj and my uncle had lost his job and my aunt was quite often ill. They needed to have more money just to live and of course, my father paid them to take care of me. I didn't think that was really fair because my uncle and his family were always at our home whenever there was a holiday or family celebration.

I could see that I wouldn't be staying there with them much longer because my uncle was having so much financial difficulty. But that school was very difficult for me. I had to study Latin, Polish, Ukrainian and German and we went to school from eight am until two pm each day and from eight to twelve on Saturday where we had to study gym, art and music.

I remember one day in the sixth grade, we were now all about twelve years old and the music teacher said to us, "Kids, you must be quiet because we are going to teach you music." My mother was a beautiful singer and a piano player, and when my father was younger, he played the violin. All my relatives were quite talented musicians, but I wasn't.

It was decided that they were going to form a choir and they put all of us kids in their choir. We sang and practiced many times and then the teacher held up her hand and stopped us. He looked at all of us and asked, "Who is it that sings so badly?" I didn't say anything but finally they realized it was me and they pulled me out of the choir. I was so ashamed because everyone knew it was me. The teacher took me aside and said to me, "Marusia, please don't sing out loud. Just move your mouth and pretend as if you are singing." Okay, I knew then that I was no good at singing either. So, from that point on, whenever we had choir practice and the teacher looked at me, I'd open my mouth and pretend I was singing too. At least the teacher didn't throw me out. I stayed with that damn choir and pretended I was singing.

I must have been tone deaf because I couldn't tell a waltz from a hymn. I remember my poor father's brother trying to teach me music for a whole year when he lived with us, and one day, he shook his head and said, "Marusia, you will never learn music."

Anyway, when I went home that Christmas, my father took me aside and told me that I could not stay with my aunt and uncle anymore. He told me that I would have to finish out the year with them and then he would decide what to do with me. He decided that I would have to go to a Ukrainian Catholic School in Lviv owned by Basilian Sisters and that was the very best school in our area. This school was considered to be the *crème-de-la-crème*.

Then he told me some very good news. He felt that he was going to be reassigned to a very, very excellent village that was close to Lviv where I would be going to school. He didn't tell me why I would have to change schools but I found that out later on.

25

My mother had a cousin who lived in Lviv and he lived very close to my school in the Ukrainian metropolis. He was a professor and a journalist and his wife was a piano teacher. They had three children and the middle girl became my best friend when I went to school in Lviv. They also had another child about eight years younger than me and an older son in medical school.

My father moved to a wonderful place. The new parish was owned by a local landowner and my father went to see him to get help. Well, that landowner liked my father and he got the parish just before Christmas.

That wealthy landowner also had a very large agricultural school for farm boys, who after seven years of local schooling, could go to this school. This couple was my parents' age but they had no children and they were very social. My parents used to get together with them quite often and they would laugh and have such good times. He had a brother who owned a large farm a few miles from our village. The brother had a wife and two girls and one of the girls was ready to go to study with me in Lviv.

By now, I was still in the gymnasium. I was quite good in art and gymnastics. My mother bought me a pair of skates and my aunt would take me and my cousins to skate and I became very good at that too.

At this time, my cousin Doris was again in jail and her brother was about sixteen years old, and I'm not sure, but I think Doris convinced him to join the Ukrainian underground. And because my aunt was still so sick, that house was not a happy place for me, so I went home to the new parish.

That new parish house was gorgeous and it was located at the top of a hill. It was surrounded by beautiful orchards, beautiful trees, and beautiful stables. In one year, my father got about twenty-four cows and horses, ducks, turkeys, geese and pigs. Really, it was a wonderful place.

Every couple of hours we had buses that stopped near our place and in a very short time we could be in Lviv. These buses stopped at six o'clock in the morning and my parents would come to Lviv to visit me, and by two o'clock in the afternoon, they were once again back home.

At that time, that parish needed a priest and they received many applications, but my father was the lucky man. He was the one they selected and now he was very, very, *very* happy. We now had the busses that came past our home on a regular basis. We could travel to the larger cities within a matter of hours, and the roads were excellent too.

Autumn came and we had something that we called Ukrainian plums or Italian plums. This fruit was excellent for cooking and we made everything from them: pies, cakes and cookies and my mother even made preserves from them too. We had a huge garden on our land and we grew every kind of plant and vegetable that could be grown in the fertile soil of Ukraine. And we also had many honey bees. Our cellar was always full of all kinds of home-grown foods for us to eat.

There was no electricity and we didn't have refrigerators, but just beyond the house, there was a little hill and this hill had been turned into our outdoor cellar. Every year before spring arrived, the farm workers would carry sheets of ice into this little cave and this served as our refrigerator.

Looking back, it seems as though we had very little, but it's funny because we were all so happy at that time. There was electricity in Lviv but it wasn't very reliable. One minute it was on and the next minute it was off.

When we had a pig to kill, this was a very big thing. Maybe a month or so before Easter or Christmas, my father would slaughter some pigs and we would eat these all year. My father knew a man, a specialist, who would come to kill the pigs. This man really was a butcher and he could take every edible part of that poor pig and turn it into food. He used every part from the pig's ears to its toes. Nothing was ever wasted. This man would stay with us for a couple of days and they'd make bacon, liverwurst, marinated ham and baloney. Liverwurst was really his specialty, and we usually saved the marinated ham for special holidays like Easter or Christmas.

We had a storage room next to our house and my father had installed heavy wires and we could always find all kinds of foods hanging there— foods like bacon and baloney. Another food we got from the pig was fat. My mother used this fat to make her homemade doughnuts and our doughnuts were a million times better than the ones you can buy today. On January fourteenth, my father's birthday, my mother always held a big party and she always made a huge batch of her wonderful doughnuts.

But my mother's doughnuts always held a little secret. She would go out to the garden in the fall and pick all the petals off her special roses and she would use these pink or red rose petals in her cooking and preserves. I can remember going to the garden with her or our maids and she would cut off the roses, leaving a short green stem. Then she'd take them into the house where she'd rinse them off and then she'd fry them in the pig's fat, sugar and wine. I don't think that I will forget that wonderful smell as long as I live. My mother was such a wonderful cook, and even after she had come to the United States, if I said that I had cooked chicken today, she'd ask me how I had cooked it and then she'd tell me how terrible the meat really was here in the United States.

I can remember going home on vacation and seeing my mother making homemade bread. She had a baking routine and every Saturday, she made her homemade bread. She'd make apple dumplings or turnovers with the cherries she grew in our garden. Everything was always so delicious! I can tell you that in all my travels around the world to different cities, I have never tasted anything as good as her cooking.

I remember going out to her garden and picking vegetables to make relish. I would pick garlic, and large white and small red onions. She'd make fresh cucumber salad and she'd have fresh, red strawberries for us to eat too. She used to make us meringue cookies and pies and they were the best I have ever eaten and we usually had these wonderful foods every Sunday during our vacations. Sadly, I never learned how to make all of those delicious dishes.

When I was about thirteen, I always had to wear a uniform to school. And every spring when I'd return home, my mother would go with me to the store and buy me two different materials to make me two new dresses. One of the dresses was for "everyday" wear and the other was for Sunday. I always had to wear the "ugly" uniform shoes to school, so my mother took me to buy some fancy new shoes to wear at home.

There was a young girl who came from Sernyky and she was very talented in sewing. Her family was very poor and she was an orphan. In those days, a seamstress could make very good money. When I would come home on vacation, she used to come to visit my parents because

28

they always used to help her in any way they could. She would stay with us for about a month or even longer and she would sew me new dresses or alter my old ones so that I would have clothes to wear while home on vacation. This girl told my mother that I needed a bra and my mother had her sew me some. She made me a green one, a blue one, a white one and a yellow one. They were so pretty and she even sewed some lace on them. I remember that my mother had a corset but she didn't really wear it, and she only started to wear a bra when she was much older. All the village girls made their own corsets and they would use pretty lace or ribbons on them too.

I had never heard of lipsticks or makeup, and my mother kept a big secret from me. My mother was so very tiny and so dark and so beautiful that I think we must have had some Gypsy or Hungarian in our blood. My mother was so dark that people often called her a porcelain doll. She always had a lovely complexion and I think she must have used red Vaseline on her lips because she didn't have lipstick back then. My father was so handsome and he had curly blond hair and blue eyes.

When I was nearly fourteen, my aunt, who was a concert pianist and lived in the city, took her daughter, my cousin, and me to a beauty shop. At that time, nearly all the girls wore their hair in the longer braided styles that were fashionable back then. My aunt told me that she thought it was about time for me to get my hair done. I usually wore my hair in two long braids and I think the beautician cut my braids off because braids were not in style back then. And from then on, I think I had short hair.

Both of my parents were very health conscious even though, in those days, they didn't know that kids needed vitamins or really anything about our health. My brother and I had the smallpox vaccine and that was all.

I was quite well-nourished when I was a small child because they always pushed milk, eggs, salads and sweets on me. I came down with the English disease, rickets, and because of that, I had poor teeth. I didn't have any enamel on my teeth and my mother took me to a dentist when I was about eight years old. The dentist looked into my mouth and told my mother that he needed to put some fillings in my teeth. That old dentist looked just like a monster to me.

In those days, they didn't have electric dental drills, anesthesia, or anything like that. So he started to clean my teeth and put the fillings in. You have no idea how painful that procedure was. When I cried and yelled, he threatened me by saying, "Little girl, you'd better be quiet!" And can you guess what I did? He had his two big fat fingers in my mouth and I bit him so hard that he screamed and hollered. My mother was in the waiting room and he went to get her and he told her, "Your daughter is a monster and I won't work on her anymore!"

"Well, what about her teeth?" My mother asked him. "I don't care about her teeth!" He yelled back at my mother. "Look at my fingers!" And she saw that they were bleeding. She took me home and I was so glad that I didn't have to go through all the misery of having fillings in my teeth and I don't think I saw another dentist till I was about twelve.

At that time, there was a very nice, Jewish lady dentist in Stryj and my uncle took me to see her. She was so wonderful and she was so careful. I don't know how she did it, but she fixed my teeth and I didn't have to bite her fingers. My father always had very beautiful teeth and when he died at the age of eighty, he had no cavities. He was missing one tooth because during the war you couldn't go into town. Because he wanted to go into town, he told one of his superiors that his tooth was hurting him and he needed to go to the dentist, and they let him go. The dentist only asked him what tooth was bothering him and he pulled it out even though there wasn't anything wrong with that tooth. My father always told us that story.

Later on when I was about twelve or thirteen, my mother took me to a doctor and he found that I had scoliosis of the spine because my bones were so soft. This doctor told my mother that I should not carry a handbag so I had to use a backpack.

When I was in Stryj, my mother and father insisted that I go to play piano and they sent me to music school for three years and it cost them a lot of money. I did not enjoy studying the piano at all and I really couldn't understand the difference in musical arrangements. I didn't care if I was playing the Ave Maria or Yankee Doodle. To me it made no difference. After three years of teaching me, the teacher sent my parents a long letter saying that he did not want to teach me any longer because I could not learn. And after three years, I had learned nothing.

I was so glad that I did not have to go study with him any longer, and that was one of the happiest days of my life! That finished my musical career and it would have been much better for everyone if they had sent me to painting school because I loved painting and we did have painting classes in my school.

My father took me aside and told me. "Marusia, because we just moved here and your school is very expensive, I think you need to have a private tutor." My younger brother was still in grammar school in the fourth grade. Upon hearing all this, I wasn't unhappy and I wasn't happy either. I was not a good student anyway and I went to school to have a good time, not to study. But then I thought that if I had a private tutor, then maybe I wouldn't have to work so hard. I thought to myself that maybe the teacher wouldn't expect too much of me and I wouldn't have to study all the time. That was always foremost in my mind—not to study.

And guess what a "jewel" I got for a teacher! She was a graduate at the gymnasium and when she finished there, she had no money to go on to college. She was an "A" student and her older sister had married my father's best classmate. Her husband was a very successful business man and her father had died during World War One and her mother was very poor. Her mother had taken cleaning jobs to support herself and her teenage daughter.

So my father hired her to be my tutor. Can you believe it? That young girl turned my world upside down! After all the smart, educated adults who had tried to teach me all my growing up years, this young girl was the one who made me understand what all the others had been trying for years to teach me.

First of all, I loved her! She was so beautiful; she was smart and so very patient with me. I still can't understand how that young girl, who had just finished her studies at the gymnasium, could get me to understand all the things I had turned my mind against.

My uncle sent me all the books to use in her classes and she came to me and she said, "Marusia, I want you to be proud that I am your teacher. When I finish teaching you, I want them to say that I have done an excellent job. I hope that you will be good because you really don't

31

want to be good. Can you do that for me? I want you to be proud that I could make something out of you. Because right now, you are nothing! You are no good!" I looked up into her bright, brown eyes and resolved to do my very best for her and myself! She taught me all that year and I had never worked so hard.

At this time, my baby brother was now eleven and I got some skis. I was skiing like crazy and I was a very good skier. Not a good student, but a good skier and skater. It was Christmas and my grandmother was still alive and she still made homemade candies. I wouldn't help her because I was too busy. It was a couple of days after Christmas and as was the custom there, we always hung chocolate from the Christmas tree branches. So I went and I stole all the chocolate that was still hanging from the Christmas tree. When my brother saw that the chocolates were all gone, he started to cry. He yelled to our mother, "Ma, what's happened to all the chocolates? I want some chocolates!"

My mother would always say to us, "Kids, there are plenty of sweets." We had cakes, cookies, pies, everything. She wanted to save the chocolates until after Christmas and then she would remove them from the tree and divide them between my brother, myself and my uncle, because he was like a child, and for my BaBa and herself. My father would always give his share to me, and my mother would give her share to her beloved son.

Anyway, do you know what I did? I stuffed the chocolates, one after another, into my mouth and I ate like a pig. I'm surprised that I didn't get sick. I ate nearly all of them. I didn't touch the oranges but I did eat the chocolates. Then my brother started to scream and holler at me and guess what I did? I decided to lie and I said, "Why do you always try to blame me? I didn't take any chocolates!" I lied and blamed it on the maids. My conscience still bothers me about this to this very day.

My mother looked at me and she said, "Mary, how can you say that?" I looked back at my mother and said, "Well, we have all kinds of maids here and they probably stole all the chocolates!" And I felt so guilty. Those poor maids never stole anything from us. I was the one who stole. I never told anyone the real story until I was grown up and my brother had passed away.

I never got sick from eating all that chocolate and to this day, I can never have enough chocolate. If I had even five cents, I'd go and buy some chocolate candy. And you know what? I still love chocolate!

That young woman, my new teacher, I don't know what she had, but she had a way of teaching so that I could understand everything she told me. My father was still teaching me religion, and my mother was teaching me German. But my teacher knew German and she knew Ukrainian, Polish, Latin, advanced math, history and geography too. She was a real teacher.

You know, there finally came the day when I had to take the final "high" exam that would last for three or four days. My father and I went to Lviv and I stayed with my cousin once again. Do you know what? I made an "A+." The Director, who was a priest and my father's teacher in the past, came to see us and congratulated me. He said, "Do you know what? Your daughter is the smartest student that I have ever given the entrance exam to!" Now that I think about it, I was smart but nobody knew how to reach me or how to teach me. That young teacher loved me and she treated me like her younger sister.

One day when I was about fourteen, I started to have cramps and I didn't know what was going on. My mother hadn't told me anything about being a "woman". I complained to my mother that I wasn't feeling well, and she asked, "Marusia, what's wrong?" I looked at her and I cried, "My stomach hurts, I have terrible cramps! I think maybe I hurt myself, I am bleeding and I don't know what to do!"

Right away she went and got some things for me and then she told my grandmother about me and it was my grandmother who told me that this will happen every month. My grandmother was the one who told me to clean myself and what to do to take care of all that. Then, she told me about having babies. I didn't even know how a woman got pregnant!

I don't wish to embarrass my mother because she was very good to me. But when I was about fourteen years old, I went to my mother and asked her if I was pretty. My mother, instead of saying I am pretty, she said, "Mary, that's not important; it's important to be smart and good." Nobody ever said I was beautiful and that hurt my feelings because I always wanted to know that. But my brother must have been very handsome because all the women always said, "What a handsome son you have," to my mother.

Anyway, my father was so happy that I had gotten such fine grades that he went to a jeweler and bought me a beautiful watch and one for my teacher too. She had taught me so much about everything. She was a *real* teacher. She really was a "God sent" teacher.

After that, when I returned to the regular school, I was now their top student. I was always the best student in school until I finished medical school. And I owe it all to her. I now understood that there was nothing wrong with being a teacher and there was nothing wrong in being a student who seemed to know something. I went from being a "D" student in math to being an all "A" student in all my subjects.

Now I loved going to school and I had a very good time. I was now about fourteen and my brother was still in grammar school, but when I went to Lviv, he was still staying with my aunt who was very sick. My mother was afraid that my brother was still too young to go to the city school, therefore, they sent my brother to live with my uncle and to go to school in Stryj. I think that he stayed with them for two years until my aunt died, then he needed a private tutor for one year and he stayed there till nineteen thirty-nine when World War Two started.

I had another uncle and aunt in Lviv and they had three children. The oldest was the son who was in medical school and that was really something because the Poles did not accept Ukrainians at medical school. Their middle girl, Hala, was my age and she became my best friend. They had another daughter, Oksana, who was younger than me. She was only ten years old. I stayed with my aunt and uncle the longest of any place because I really loved staying in their home.

Then my aunt found a place for me to stay that was across the street. The woman was a widow of a professor-priest and she had six grown-up children. Mostly I was in school, and after school I would go to visit my cousin, Hala, whom I loved and she loved me too. We were very, very good friends. Her mother was very nice and her mother would take us to the movies. Her husband, my uncle-cousin was a very smart man. He was a journalist and he taught at the gymnasium also. As a newspaper man, every once in a while he used to get free tickets and my aunt used to take us to the movies. As for me, that was paradise, a heaven in this world. We also had American movies. At that time, the movies were all black and white and so grainy and horrible. It was such an early time for movies and the technology was so primitive.

Then a miracle happened. One day, Hala's mother, my aunt, came to see me and she told me, "I have a big surprise. Now you are old enough, you should learn how to dance." She took us to dance class which was being taught by Ukrainian high-school teachers. These teachers were very strict and we couldn't even talk to the boys who were sixteen or seventeen years old. The teachers taught the boys to bow to us and we were waltzing or dancing the polka and I was very happy because some of the boys were very good looking. This was one of the nicest times in my life. I loved my dancing classes and my parents paid for me to go. I used to go dancing there once or twice a week and I loved it.

Hala and I always had a very good time but she didn't attend the same school as me. Hala attended a Ukrainian school but her school wasn't a Catholic school, it was another private school. But every day after class I got to see her.

I liked my teachers but I could barely handle all the studies. I had a lot of physics, chemistry and anatomy. These were very difficult subjects, but I really needed to study them for my career. I hated math and I thank God for my uncle Paul, my father's youngest brother who studied engineering in Lviv. He would come, not once, but twice a week and he helped me to better understand math. But even with all his help, math was still very difficult for me. I had to study every waking moment.

My girlfriend, my landlord's daughter, also attended the gymnasium with me, but she didn't want to go on to higher education. She wanted to be a farmer, so she applied to study agriculture. But the school officials told her that if she wanted to study that subject, she would have to go to another school for those classes. She made plans to go to Warsaw but it was September, nineteen thirty-nine and the war started and she has to give up all her plans.

That year was a very hard year for me to have to study so much, even though I had a very nice place to study. My brother was still in Stryj with my aunt and uncle. By now, my aunt was so ill that she could hardly get out of bed and walk around. I don't know why they still kept my brother with them but they did. My cousin, their daughter, was still in jail and their son was now in his last year of high school in Stryj.

Now it is Easter and I loved to go out and dance. Dancing was another thing that I loved besides art and skating, and the land owner's wife used to have big parties for Easter and Christmas and they invited all of us. They had a few nephews, young boys who came to visit them, which of course I didn't mind, and the lady used to play very beautiful music on her piano. We used to dance and I was very happy that my father had been selected for that new parish.

The lady where I stayed had a very lovely family. One son was a lawyer and another was an economist. A third son went to Salzburg, Austria and later became a Catholic priest. This widowed lady also had three daughters. The oldest one was a secretary in a Ukrainian bank, another was studying medicine and she finished her studies before the end of World War Two. Another girl studied economics. I stayed with that family about two years.

Then I met a girl who was two or three years older than me, in the gymnasium. Her parents were both teachers and she had one sister. And she said to me, "Why do you stay with this old lady and so many people?" She thought where I stayed was not a nice place. She told me, "Marusia, why don't you come stay with me next year?" And she found a very nice big house with a young couple who had no children. The home was beautiful and overlooked a park. I loved it there because my room was much nicer than the one I had.

I brought my parents to see my new room and my mother didn't mind but my father said he would have to check everything. The lady was the daughter of a judge and she was teaching piano in a college conservatory. This lady was a beautiful piano player and she gave private lessons from morning until night. But this didn't bother me because the room we had was located on the side of the building.

Now it is nineteen thirty-eight, I finished four years of gymnasium, and then they changed from eight to four years of classic studies. If you wanted to be a priest, you could choose to study classics. You had to study the humanistic if you wanted to be a physician, or a pharmacist. I finished the four classes and I was an "A" student. Like I said before, nothing came to me easily and I had to study very hard.

Our lyceum, a secondary school, had a humanistic for two years and I chose this place because I thought I might go on to study medicine.

My mother was very much against this because she had never seen a female physician. And if there were any women who were doctors, they were old maids and who would want to marry a woman physician? These were my plans but I didn't know what was going to happen.

I loved it there, I had much more freedom and there wasn't so many people living in that house. The food was lovely at the new house and I loved everything. I was so happy that I had moved there. My girlfriend, the seamstress, came to stay at my parent's house for a week or so and she sewed me some lovely dresses and we had a lovely summer's visit.

My new landlady came from a family of five or six children and she had a brother who studied law. He was so short I don't think that he was even four feet tall. He was not too bad looking and he was always after me. He was always trying to teach me something or help me with my homework, and I didn't like him and I tried to run away. One day there was a school dance and I didn't go to school dances. Well, this boy came and begged me to go to the school dance with him. This was a love affair that wasn't. The more he bothered me, the more I didn't like him. He was about nineteen and not for me.

Please don't misunderstand me, but I have decided that when I write my memoirs, I want to stay away from politics as much as I can. I was not involved in politics.

My father found out that the Poles had formed a concentration camp. And they were sending our young men and women there. My big love was books, studying, and nothing else. But I could not go about with my eyes closed. Our school was very quiet and we didn't know anything was going on around us. Our teachers didn't discuss anything about politics or the war. We really were not allowed to discuss anything political in school because the Poles around us were beginning to become very suspicious of Ukrainians. Every year there would be more jailing of young people. And our underground-boys, who had no jobs, burned the Polish farmer's fields of hay and some of their houses, and that was a big no, no and the Poles were becoming very angry with us. Hitler and Stalin were just beginning to come into power. It was now about nineteen thirty-five or thirty-six and the Poles tried to find and arrest all the young boys.

The Poles were becoming crazy and they had signs everywhere saying "Watch Out For German Spies"! Everywhere you could smell the coming war and our stupid politicians, Ukrainians, didn't know anything. Some were waiting for Hitler because we had been told that he would come to Ukraine and make us independent. We didn't know that Hitler was killing people everywhere he went. We didn't know about those atrocities; we were even more afraid of the Russians. We were so afraid of them that we were even afraid to mention the word "Russian".

Now, the Poles started to become afraid of Hitler. They were afraid that Hitler might take over Poland. The more they were afraid, the worse they treated the minorities. They didn't know who to trust, and everyone was suspected of being a German spy.

My father's best friend had been a soldier in the Ukrainian Army when we were at war from nineteen eighteen until nineteen twenty-one and the fall of the Austrian Empire when the Poles took over. That man stayed in the city of Prague, Czechoslovakia and then he married and worked there. He came to visit his ailing mother, and he and his family stayed at our home. They were very lovely people and he proposed to my father that later I should go with them to Prague. We made plans that when I graduated from liceum, I would go to study medicine there.

Ukrainians were treated very well there, and because I was a very good student I wouldn't have any problems to be accepted to medical school. I was more than happy to go with them. My grandmother didn't say anything; my mother probably didn't like it because I must go away to Prague and I was so young, but I was very excited. I told all my friends that I was going to Prague to study medicine. Maybe I shouldn't have talked so much because everything changed after that.

In the village where my father was the landlord, there was a younger Ukrainian couple who lived next door to us and they loved to see us having such a good time. They had no children and they loved watching us play. Their house was always full of younger people; their nieces, nephews and cousins were always there. That lady loved us and she always invited us to come and visit. There were many young, good looking college boys, and boy oh boy didn't Hala, my cousin, and I have fun! That lady played piano and she always encouraged us to dance.

In nineteen thirty-seven, my girlfriend's mother died of a heart attack and she was the one who went to the same school as me in Lviv. She would now come to my house and stay. Josephine or (Minia) was very nice and very friendly but she was not a beauty. Her grandmother was German but her grandfather was from Kazakhstan and she had oriental features, which was a little bit strange to us because we didn't normally see oriental people. But she was a beautiful singer.

Minia would come to stay at her aunt's and that landlady lived next to my father's house. She and Hala and I were always together and the boys were there too. We had a whole house full of young people. And guess what we had? We had a nice field behind the stable and we played volleyball every day during our summer vacation.

My cousin, Oleh, was two years older and he and my brother used came to stay and we used to play volley ball too, and I became very good in sports! I played as well as the boys. We were four or five girls and we would play volleyball all the time when we were all on vacation. We didn't cook, we didn't clean, all we did was to play games and have a good time.

My mother always gave the volleyball to Myron but he was really too young to play with us. But my father always made sure that he would go out and play. My grandmother would call for all of us to come and have a little snack of tea or milk and cookies or sandwiches. Sometimes she would invite everyone to stay for supper but usually it was just a snack. We didn't drink coffee, only my parents did. Sometimes we did have hot chocolate though. I don't remember drinking coffee until I was much older.

My father made all kinds of wine. He used the alcohol made from honey for his drinks, and boy was that good. I was not allowed to drink, but if nobody was watching, I would steal a little drink every now and then. His wine was sweet and good and I remember when I was about fourteen years old, my father would make a big crock of wine. He would leave it to ferment until it was ready. He used to make all kinds of different wines using the fruits and berries on our farm. Apple, cherry, strawberry, blueberry, blackberry and current wines are what I can remember. Sugar wasn't rationed but it was very expensive. Father would make sugar from sweet beets too. Nobody ever bought anything at our home. My father was very well organized and there wasn't anything he couldn't do or make.

When we had too much of anything from the farm, my father would take it to the farming co-operative to sell. We never bought bread, butter, milk or cheese. Sometimes though, we did buy a special sugar for coffee or cooking. We usually used honey instead of refined sugar.

We did have to buy kerosene for our lamps because we didn't have electricity, and we had to buy salt. We didn't buy any shampoo; we used egg yolks to wash our hair and it was lovely too. If the older women wanted to color their gray hair, they used walnut leaves. After the leaves had been boiled, they would rinse their hair with the water. If they wanted to have a reddish color for their hair, they used red onion leaves. I never saw real shampoo until I was thirteen or fourteen and was living in Lviv. I had to go to a school dance and I went to a beautician. She put this stuff in my hair and when I asked what it was, she told me "shampoo". I couldn't understand what that word was and I thought she said, "Champagne".

It was now the spring of nineteen thirty-nine and I was ready to go to my second year of liceum in the autumn. Then my aunt died at the age of forty-eight and my uncle arranged her funeral. It was a huge affair, but her daughter was not there because she was still in jail. My uncle and his son stayed with us all that summer. My uncle cried all the time and was so depressed.

I remember one time when we were eating supper and we had about twelve or fifteen guests there with us and my father made the comment, "Maybe the Russians will come." At that time, nobody knew how terrible the Russians really were. I can tell you that if you had to live under the Devil's control, it never would have been as terrible as living under the Russians control. Now you can smell the unrest in Poland, and the Polish soldiers were walking on the streets all over and they were always increasing in numbers.

At the beginning of August, all the families, six or seven of them, always used to go to a shrine in the nearby mountains of Univ. It was about an hour's drive for them using horses. There was a beautiful monastery and a shrine with the statues of Mary and Jesus. There was a huge, beautiful church and a wonderful library, and all the families would go to confession and communion. People came from all over our country every year to stop and pray there. This place was famous for its healing powers and all kinds of people traveled there to be blessed and cured of any and all injuries.

We had made plans to go to Univ and my mother had made all kinds of sandwiches with chicken and cold ham and coffee and apple juice. It was really going to be a beautiful trip and a picnic for us. We got as far as Peremyshlany and then we saw a whole bunch of Polish police and they stopped us. They came up to my father and asked where we were going. We told them that we were traveling to Univ and they told us that we were crazy. They told us that we were going to have a war and that they may need our horses. So we turned around and went back home, and in just two weeks the war started between Germany and Poland.

The Poles were completely unprepared and very ill-equipped for war. The Poles had only horses to fight with and the Germans had tanks. The Germans also had many planes and the Poles had only a few. It was now September first and the war only lasted one week. It was called a "Blitzkrieg" or a "Lightening War."

Before the war broke out, the Poles were always running around telling everyone how they were going to annihilate the Germans, but they were such fools. And we Ukrainians were naive and stupid too, because we thought that when the Germans came, they would save us and allow us to become independent. We believed the German propaganda that Hitler would free all the countries and set us free.

Anyway, from the Black Sea to the Baltic Sea, fifty million people were dancing because they believed that Hitler was so good. One day, Polish soldiers came running into our village like crazy, screaming that the Germans were coming. The Poles ran away into the Carpathian Mountains to Hungary and to Italy. They couldn't fight and so they ran away.

My father listened to the radio and they were predicting that within a week, everybody would gain their independence, but that was not true. It was all propaganda. The Poles fell down. We thought that within a week or so, the Germans would come, but nobody was coming. To our horror, the Russians made a "non-aggression" treaty with the Germans. The Germans took West Poland and the Russians took the West Ukraine. For us, that was like somebody had shot us because we thought we knew how bad the Russians really were

* * * * *

For a few paragraphs I want to digress back to nineteen eighteen to explain what happened previously between Ukraine and Russia.

In nineteen eighteen, Ukrainians were trying to become independent but they were not strong enough. The Poles were fighting for their independence too. The Russians were fighting for communism and everybody thought that if you fought the Russian Czar, then everybody would gain their independence. But that was not true; it was all propaganda. In Ukraine they only had independence from nineteen eighteen until nineteen twenty-two and then the Russians destroyed them too.

In nineteen twenty-four, Ukraine became a "Soviet Republic" of the U.S.S.R., the United Soviet Socialist Republic. Everyone was told that all the war-torn countries would now be free and could have their own government, language and even their own army. They would all be "independent states." Everyone believed this propaganda and again, we were all so naive. Our Ukraine fell, and the Communists took over and destroyed our Ukraine.

The first thing the Russians did when they became the "Communists" in the Central and the East Ukraine was to make the farms co-ops. Our farmers were not used to this way and they didn't want to join the co-ops. So, they started to fight the Russians. The Russians took all their food away and in our country alone, over six million Ukrainians died from starvation. The farmers even used to strip the bark from the trees and then boil it and eat it. Little dead children were lying in the streets with their bellies swollen from hunger and lack of food. Once Stalin, who was Georgian, even invited a big Ukrainian concert singer to his dacha. He plied all of his guests with wonderful drinks and food and he ordered his soldiers to take all of his Ukrainian guests to his prison where they killed them all.

Stalin was so hated that he didn't dare to even taste his food until another person had eaten some of it first. His first wife died from food poisoning but he didn't die because he was so smart. He remarried and he was a womanizer and a sex maniac. He was even worse than The Devil.

* * * * *

Now it is September, nineteen thirty-nine and my father learned that war had started between the Germans and the Poles. At this time, my mother's niece Doris and her fiancé had been arrested by the Poles for being spies and she was held in prison about a year. They stayed in the Polish prison until the Communists came and then they ran away. They were very lucky they were not killed.

Then Doris came back to Stryj. She took my uncle and her brother and they ran away. They didn't know where they were going to go to but they knew that if they stayed, the Russians would kill them. I found out later that they really were a part of the Ukrainian underground.

In our village we did have some Communist sympathizers and they made some big "Welcome" signs for the Communists. When the first Russians came into our village, they were well-dressed officers, riding in open cars. After they had passed through, then came the regular foot soldiers and what a mess they were! They were very poorly dressed and they looked like bums. Some only had on part of a uniform and many were not even shaved. Some wore house slippers and some were bare foot. They did not look like anyone's idea of a "conquering army". We Ukrainians were all standing quietly and we were all shocked when we saw how poorly they were dressed.

Now all our people who knew of the war between the Poles and the Germans were afraid. Now we were being told that we were "free" because Stalin was brighter than the sunshine. Stalin was a savior sent from God above. We were really lucky in a way because they didn't bother too much with our Ukrainian people. At the beginning, they didn't put us all in jail.

About a week or two of the Russians being in our village, my father was scared "shitless" because he knew that as a priest, he would be persecuted. Then we heard a big speech on the radio and then the next week the newspapers started to come again. Then the propaganda began once more about the Ukrainians being free and that the West Ukraine people would not be persecuted any more by the Poles. Now Ukrainians can now go to school for free; Ukrainians will have the best positions in the universities; all professors who have been persecuted by the Poles will have very good jobs; all Poles will be directors of factories. It was all propaganda, propaganda, propaganda.

Many of the village people came to my father and said that the Russians will not harm us—that we will all have very good positions. My father looked at them like they were insane. He told them that they were crazy to believe all that stuff. Didn't they know how the Russians had treated others? But our village people didn't want to listen—that's how brainwashed all those people were.

I didn't want to go to Lviv because I was very scared. After about a month of occupying our village, the Russians went to my uncle in Lviv and arrested him along with many other top Ukrainians. I don't know how they knew that these people were our elite, but they did.

In the meanwhile, the Russians ordered all the schools' patriot teachers and all the nuns and priests in West Ukraine to leave the schools, and they all ran away. That October I went to Lviv to find out about school and when it was going to reopen. I needed to go back to school and now there was no gymnasium or liceum school, only tenth grade. There were now no Latin, German or Polish languages, only Ukrainian and Russian. No anatomy, only chemistry and math.

When my uncle was arrested with all the other top professors, my aunt was very scared. My brother and I needed to go to school in Lviv so we stayed with the same lady where we had stayed before.

The Russians stole everything that they could find. Then one day, they came to my father's house. There were only a few soldiers and they looked like tramps that carried guns. They told my mother to give them all of her gold. My mother didn't have very much gold. She had to open her drawers or they would kill her. She had a bracelet and one or two little brooches and a set of pearls. She gave the soldiers a few American dollars and a few gold coins my father had given her. Now you know how terrible the Russians really were. The Russians left us two cows, one horse, and a few chickens. The rest of the animals, they took away with them.

We had very little food but they didn't take that. My father thought they would probably throw us out of our home, or make us move into the village and then take everything out of our house. We knew that if we brought any food with us to Lviv and on the way back on the train, then the soldiers would kill you.

Somehow one night, my father slaughtered a large pig and he and his good friend put all that meat in his horse's wagon, and using the small streets and alleys, they brought it all to us. That food lasted us nearly two months until Christmas. I was never very religious, but when the Communists came, I became very religious.

Now, if you went to Lviv, there were long lines on every street. People were lining up to get whatever others were selling. They would try to sell you shoes in size eight or ten, or clothes. If you went into the city at twelve o'clock at night, maybe by eight o'clock the next morning you will still be waiting there. Sometimes, you might be lucky to get a loaf of bread or a piece of meat. You never knew what was coming. One man might have a pair of boots in size twelve and you might need a size six. We would exchange them until we found a size that fit.

I never felt sorry for the Poles but then I noticed a truck full of women being sent to a Siberian detention camp in Russia. I learned of women and children being taken away, and when the Russians found out that a husband was a high-ranking officer, you were in big, big trouble. You would be sent to a labor camp in Siberia or Kazakhstan.

My aunt began sending my two cousins, one sixteen and the other girl was ten, to school, never thinking that something might happen to her. She was a piano teacher. And one day, the soldiers came to her home and gave my aunt and the girls two hours to pack their belongings. They also took what they could from the home which wasn't much, and one soldier told my girlfriend Hala, "Never mind putting your clothes in there. Put some bread in there because you will starve if you don't." Then they took them to the train station and put all the women and children on the trains. They traveled for days and days before they reached Kazakhstan.

Somehow, they were able to write me a letter about how horrible their life now was. In Kazakhstan they stayed in a cave in the ground and the weather was so very hot because of the continental climate and the winter was really brutal there. During the day, they were taken to a huge factory where they were forced to make cinder blocks with their bare feet. Their feet were so sore and red that they could barely walk. They had some food but the food was really horrible. They were kept in that terrible place until Stalin died.

When Khrushchev came into power, he was part Ukrainian and he wasn't so bad as a Communist. He allowed all women and children to return to Ukraine. He wouldn't give them money to pay for their way home, but my aunt found someone in Ukraine to give her the money and they came home. But once home, they could not return to school, they could not have a job, all they could do was manual labor in Lviv.

Hala returned to Lviv and she had horrible luck. She married a man and they had one child. After that, he became an alcoholic and he left her. About ten years later, he came back and their child begged to have his father back. And like a stupid fool, she took him back. He was already very sick from drinking and after about a year, he became paralyzed. Hala went back to school and finished accounting classes and found a job in a meat factory as an accountant. Some of the employees would steal some of the meat, knowing that if they were caught, they would be killed. She told me that she hid the stolen meat up her dress and she did it to survive. Her father died in Siberia in the gold mines under horrible conditions; he was only about fifty years of age. In the meantime, her husband that she took back had a severe stroke, and for ten years she had to nurse him until he died.

I had another cousin on my mother's side. That cousin was an only child and he was lucky because his parents were able to send him to Warsaw, the capitol of Poland, to study journalism. He finished just before the war came in nineteen thirty-nine and he returned home. When he got back, the Russians took over. And I can say, in the beginning, they gave Ukrainians good positions, the ones who were not afraid and the ones who were not arrested. He was young, only twenty-four or twenty-five and he was hired as vice-president of the radio station and he also worked as a radio announcer. He had just married but his good luck didn't stay with him very long. His mother loved him to pieces and she helped him any way she could. His parents had a nice home and they gave him some furniture to help him furnish his apartment. After two or three weeks of being a radio announcer using the Ukrainian language, the Communists came and became his supervisor and took his vice-president job away. He told his mother and father that he thought that man was very, very nice and maybe he should invite that man to his home for supper. Well, this was a very bad mistake.

My cousin was newly married and had a very pretty wife and he invited his new boss and his wife to their home. Of course his boss had never seen such a lovely home because the Communists didn't have nice homes. My cousin gave his guests a lovely dinner party with good food and wines and they had a wonderful evening together.

About two or three weeks later, the KGB came to arrest him. The KGB never wore uniforms; they were always dressed very informal. You really couldn't tell them from the other people on the streets. The KGB was always very nice when they came to arrest you. They would say, "We would like you to come to our station, we would like to ask you some questions." There was no mention of "police". They took him to jail and arrested him. About two or three days later, the KGB came to his apartment and told his poor wife to move out. She was only allowed to take one suitcase and that was it. After two or three weeks, they found out that his former boss liked his apartment, so he took their apartment with all their furniture and moved in.

Many years later we found out that my cousin had been sent to Siberia for ten or fifteen years because the Communists said he was a spy or their enemy. When he finally returned, he was about forty-five years old and somebody killed him on the streets of Lviv. His mother and father died before he was killed. But this random killing was really nothing new. The Communists were doing that to everybody.

That autumn when the Communists came, we had to go to school. My brother had to go to school too, and he still had three years left. My father brought us to a nice, young couple where I had stayed before. Now the problem is, they don't want money because money was not worth anything at that time. The problem was that it was so difficult to find food; my poor father had to bring us food. If you only had a sandwich or some little food, nobody would touch you. But if you had a suitcase full of food, then you were a smuggler and smugglers would be killed instantly. Smugglers just like the monks, priests or nuns were considered non-desirable people by the Communists.

Even today I don't know how my father did it. I remember one day in autumn, it was November and already very cold. That night, my brother and I were staying at that lady's home and there was a knock on the door. We opened the door and there was a man dressed as a farmer standing there. It was my father! Of course he would have been afraid to dress as a priest. My father and his friend brought us a full carriage of food for us to eat. What a father wouldn't do for his children! He could have been shot down like a dog and he put his life on the line for us. That food lasted us for two months until Christmas.

Another thing that the Russians used to do: I had a girlfriend who had a sister and a month or two after she had graduated from high school, her sister was arrested. One day when we were in class, someone knocked on the door, and the superintendent, who was a Communist, brought two men into the class and they took my girlfriend out. Later on we found out that she had been arrested also. We never really knew what happened to her; she was probably killed. She was only sixteen and her sister was in jail and maybe she talked and told them something. I never saw that poor girl again.

Then one day some of my older friends told me, "Marusia, when you walk with anyone on the streets, don't ever talk about anything bad about the Communists. You know how girls might say, "Gee, because of the Communists, we don't have food, or stockings." "We cannot dress up." When the Communists saw two girls or a couple of boys walking on the street, they would come and take one of them aside and ask them what they were talking about. Then they'd question the other one too to see if they both gave the same answer. God forbid if you didn't. If you told them something different, then you were in serious trouble. That's why, when we used to go out together, we only talked about the weather or about our school or homework. We never talked about the Communists because we never knew whom we could trust.

Our class from the gymnasium became Class Number Ten because we had graduated. The Communists took away Latin and German. We had only Ukrainian, Russian, math and certain chemistry classes. Now we are about two years behind where we used to be and it is no longer a progressive school.

One day some of my girlfriends approached me very secretly in school and told me that one of our former priests wants to teach us religion privately. We were used to being taught by priests in our former school days but this was different. So, I decided to join them. We were about six or ten girls that the priest felt he could trust, and about once a week we had a lesson secretly in our church basement. Well, that only lasted about a month or two and somebody from our class informed the KGB and they came and arrested that poor priest. We never saw him again.

Then came our first Christmas under communism. Boy, when I came home, what a difference! We didn't travel too much because the trains were always full of people and traveling was always very bad. Nothing was like before. My mother didn't go into Lviv very often and I hadn't seen her since the fall. My mother was only thirty-nine and my father was about forty-four and I saw how my parents had aged. I kept looking at them and I couldn't believe what the war and Communist occupation had done to them. They were very down, very thin, and very depressed. My mother was dressed like a farm girl, her hair wasn't fixed and that was a shock to me. She had always been elegantly dressed with her hair done, an elegant lady. My father was so upset, he had lost a lot of weight and he had always been so well-nourished. He had been always well-dressed and so handsome. Now they looked like they were sixty years old.

And my poor grandmother, I couldn't even recognize her. She had shrunk so much and she was so skinny. I knew she couldn't last too much longer. She was about seventy-three years old and she looked like she was a hundred. What the Communists and their occupation of our beloved country had done to those poor people.

Christmas in the past had always been so joyous and I told my mother that Christmas was now so sad. My brother had come home with me and there were no maids, no farm workers. There was just one girl who would still come and she was afraid because nobody was allowed to have maids. That girl would come secretly to help my mother. We only had one or two cows and maybe one horse left. Only a few chickens were left for us. Nearly everything had been taken from us. The Communists would tell the priests that they had more than enough and then they would take everything from them. And my mother used to constantly warn my father to only say his prayers and not complain to anyone about the Communists; we didn't know who we could trust.

The Communists told my father that he couldn't stay too much longer in the parish house because they wanted to make it into a school or a little hospital because that house was too big for just a parish priest and his wife.

Somehow, they always told my father all these things but they didn't do anything to him. I think they left him alone because he always treated everybody the same and he was always so kind to everyone.

Our Christmas was so sad. We had very little food and my mother had made borsht and very little else. I was glad to leave with my brother and go back to school, and we packed our suitcases with what little food they could give us and we returned to school.

The Communists were arresting people everywhere and putting them on big trucks and filling the trains and sending them to detention camps in Siberia or to Kazakhstan. We could see all the sad women and small children crying when I went to school. There was no such thing as "human rights" at that time, not for anyone. One of my uncles, Hala's father, died in a coal mine in Siberia.

School was easy for me that year and I graduated with all A's. And there were no parties, no nothing for us. I was so sad; it was the spring of nineteen forty. A short time before my graduation from high school, my Aunt Nela, the mother of my cousin whose son was a radio announcer who had been arrested, came to see me to tell me that my grandmother had died. My aunt told me to go and tell my principal that my grandmother had died and I needed to attend her funeral on Saturday and Sunday. The principal didn't agree to that and he said, "What! She was a very old woman and ready to die. They just need to bury her and that's it." He wouldn't allow me to go. I cried and cried and one teacher told my principal, "Hey, if that was your grandmother, wouldn't you want to go and say goodbye to her?" So he finally gave in and let me go, but I could only stay one day. Only a few people came and I cried so much. The funeral was very poor because so many could not come, but some of the older villagers still came to pay their respects.

I returned to school and when Easter came I didn't dare to go home. I would have had to go by train, and the train cars were always so full of people and their belongings, you could not even squeeze in. I remember that some of the villagers came to visit me and brought me some babka and other treats my mother had made for me. So, just like Christmas, I had a horrible, horrible Easter.

The German commissioner came to Lviv and registered all the German people. Our neighbor, a Ukrainian landowner and his brother with their families, was registered in Lviv by the German commissioner because of their German ancestry, and they were sent to Germany. Communists turned his land into "state" land and everything was demolished. Their house was ransacked and everything was taken away. That landowner had another brother who was a senator and a prominent person, he was arrested with Hala's father and he died in prison.

My brother still had two more years till he graduated and I had decided that I wanted to study medicine. Under the Communist regime, if one is a sympathizer against the Communists, all will be taken and your whole family will be destroyed. I told my father about my plan to apply to medical school. So when I went to apply, the man who was taking the applications to the university asked me what my father did. I knew it was no use to lie, and because my father was a priest, I was not accepted. He told me to get out of there before I was arrested. I was very brokenhearted.

So I began to think about what else I could do. I knew German quite well and I knew Ukrainian, so I went to study to be a teacher of the Ukrainian and German languages. I applied and I was accepted, and for a whole year I studied philosophy, German and the Ukrainian languages. And I also had to study the Russian history and all about Stalin and how many times he went into battle. We had to study about Russian history and the Bolsheviks ad-nauseam.

The second year of my studies, everything became worse and worse. The Russians thought that everyone from the West Ukraine must be a spy. It was about nineteen-forty and the Russians declared war against Finland. Now there was mobilization of all the West Ukraine, some they killed and some went to jail. Because of the war with Finland, they have a good excuse to mobilize everyone. The teacher in my village had a young son who was about eighteen or nineteen and almost blind, they even mobilized him, and after about three weeks he was killed.

We Ukrainians thought that within a week, Finland would be defeated. But no, the Finns were very brave fighters and they fought against the Russians. It seems logical to think that the Finns got munitions from Germany. The Finns were well-dressed and had plenty of guns and military equipment. Finland was a very small country so how could they fight against the Russians who were so big and so strong? The Russians were thinking that if they lost the war against Finland, it would be a great shame to them so they agreed to sign a peace treaty.

Now there are Communists everywhere with propaganda. Everyone was saying "Stalin is the best." "Stalin is the greatest." "Stalin is God!" Russian propaganda was rampant. We were told that under communism everybody works, everybody has money. It was all propaganda.

Secretly, we found out that on the severely cold Finnish front, some of the United Soviet Socialist soldiers had no shoes, no stockings, and no gloves. Many died from gunshots but most of them perished from freezing because it was so cold there. That war lasted not quite a year, and the Russians stopped the war and they spread propaganda that they, the Russians, felt sorry for the Finns. Everything put out by the Russians was just a pack of lies, propaganda and more lies.

Now it is our second year under Russian occupation. We were really hungry. The couple where I stayed could no longer keep us in their house. They had no heat and the food they were getting from my parents was less and less. So after one year, we had to find another place to stay.

Just before the beginning of my second year of college, we finally found another place for my brother and me. It was very far away from my school and again my father agreed to give them some food so that my brother and I could stay with them. They were very, very nice and another girl joined us in their home. My father always brought us some food in suitcases. I don't know how he could do it, but he did.

If somebody had a nice farm, the Russians would take it. I began to pray all the time because everything was becoming horrible and I was very worried for my father. My father really was an angel because he always helped everyone. The Russians would take some of the people in the villages and send them off to detention camps and take all of their belongings.

Then I went to the university and my father was always afraid that they would come and arrest me. A woman would come to help my parents but the Communists would not allow anyone to have a maid.

If they did, they would be considered an aristocrat. So she would only come in the late afternoons or evenings. And my father told the maid that in case he and my mother were arrested, she was to send me a letter to let me know what had happened to my parents. I really was expecting to see her anytime because the arrests had escalated not only in our villages but all over West Ukraine as well, especially after the Finnish War had ceased.

In nineteen forty one, the Finnish War was soon ending. I was studying very hard and because I was an "A" student at the university, I earned a scholarship. I received a little money; it was not very much but it helped.

Now, as hard as it was, it was almost spring and my father came to see me. I almost couldn't recognize him because he had been always a very, very elegant man and he was always spotless as a priest. He came dressed like an old farmer, very, very dirty and looking like an old beggar. I asked him why he looked like that. He looked at me and said, "Well if I go out as a priest, they will say that I am bourgeois and I will be arrested."

Then he told me that he had some very big news. He didn't talk to me in the house; he waited until we were outside on the street. He said it looks good for us Ukrainians, but it doesn't look good for the Russians. He told me that it looks like the Germans want to fight the Russians. I didn't know much about politics, and then I thought, *if the Germans come, they are from the West and logically speaking that might be good for us.* We always thought that the Germans were very cultured and my father always praised them. This was before World War One. I always thought that if the Russians had been smart, and built a middle class, the Communist Party would not have been able to gain power.

My father thought that if the German's came and took over Ukraine, we will be free and maybe Hitler will make the Ukrainians independent. We didn't know anything about what was going on and we didn't realize how uninformed we were when it came to politics and propaganda. But we didn't dare to ask anybody else because we were too afraid. There were no German newspapers or any way we could learn about what was happening. And the Russian newspapers only wrote good things that were happening to them. The average people were told nothing about what was really going on in the world. My father always thought that maybe Hitler would come and free us from "those devils".

Then my father told me some very bad news. He said that once in a while when he preaches at a mass, he's certain that there were Communists there to arrest him. He told me that he doubted that he would last longer than a few more months and he, too, would be arrested.

Because my father was so smart, he had been made a Dean of all Priests at a very young age. And now my father was worried because he was a dean, and they, the Russians, were arresting priests. He told me that maybe he cannot stay in the parish house any longer. Perhaps he should abandon that house and go to live in the woods with some of his friends.

I was so stupid; I told my father that he shouldn't worry. I told him that the Communists wouldn't touch him. He told me that he didn't want us to come visit him at the parish house because now it wasn't safe. He thought it wasn't safe for a young girl like me to come to the village or even take the train. He told me that it was better for him to visit me.

Then vacation came and I didn't want to stay in Lviv. There was nothing to eat. Food was becoming more and more scarce, and you could smell that the Russians were preparing for a war with Germany. We could see that the Russians were beginning to mobilize their troops on the western front in Lviv. There was a small airport in Lviv and every morning when we went to University, we could see the pilots training at the airport. And we figured that they were training because they will soon fight the Germans. We never said a word; we went to school and we always had to say what a wonderful life we had under communism.

Now in Lviv, there were always long, long lines for food and everything. The women would stay in the lines for three or four hours or more because they needed something. Maybe the only pair of shoes they could find was a size too large but they would buy them anyway, and later on they would trade them with someone else for a pair that fit them.

When the Communists came, everybody had to work. They gave my mother a position as a teacher in our little village. One day the Communists told my mother to tell the children to pray to God and say to him, "God, we love you and we want you to give us candy." That was pure propaganda for the children. My mother couldn't tell them no, so she did as she had been told. Later on a KGB agent would come with a big sack of candy that he would hide behind the door. He would tell the children to pray to Father Stalin and other Communist leaders for candy. Then the KGB leader would open the door and throw the candy into the room and the children thought that it was due to their prayers. Communist propaganda was everywhere we went, at home, at school, at work. It was everywhere.

Even if you were lucky enough to have a job with the Communists, if you came late to work two, three, or even four times, they would immediately arrest you and take you off to jail. And you might stay in jail one day, a month, or even years, and nobody would know where you were or what had happened to you.

In the spring of nineteen forty-one, I went home on vacation. My father told me that I had to help them in the garden that was only around our house. We had no large fields left, everything had been taken. By the end of summer it was so cold and I only had a little pair of shoes and I was nearly frozen. I had to help harvest the potatoes and the red beets. I think we only had one pig, a couple of turkeys and chickens. That was it; there was no one else to help us. My grandmother was now dead, so my mother, my brother and I helped gather the harvest. Now that my brother was older, I liked him very much and he was very good to me too.

When I went back to college for my first year, the KGB came to ask my father some questions. One time they took him to the police station but they never arrested him. My mother was always dressed as a maid and the policeman thought she was a maid. She always wore a scarf, *babushka*, around her head and didn't do her hair and she wore no makeup, and now she really looked like a maid. She told the policeman that she was just a maid and that she had just come to milk the cow. The Russian policeman said she should not work for the priest.

The Communists used to hold parties for university students, but I wasn't a Communist so I never dared to go. I would hear that one after another professor had been arrested. Some Polish professors left and they were later arrested and many of them were killed. Some of my Ukrainian professors and students were arrested, and they too, perished without a trace.

The Germans were coming, that's all we thought about. We were all waiting for them. It is easy to criticize us, but if you have two devils, you look to see which devil is better. After all, *the devil you know is better than the one you don't.* We started to notice in the newspapers every once in a while that things were beginning to change. Russians started to mobilize our young people. We could hear all the tanks and trucks going to the west. Because my father had some connections with people in the Ukrainian underground, he began hearing stories that soon there will be a war between the Russians and Germans. Now I was so worried because my brother Myron was now about the age to be drafted.

Now we began to hear the planes in the sky around our university. I was thinking that pretty soon the Russians would begin their war with the Germans because the Russians began belittling the Germans in the newspapers. The Russians began mobilizing all the young people. They arrested many of our college boys, school boys, and farm boys. Then we heard all the tanks and military vehicles going to the west to the front, we again knew the smell of war.

We didn't have any idea what Hitler or his army was really like. We had no one to tell us. We didn't know that Hitler had persecuted the Jewish people, that Hitler only wanted a "white" race and he had all the gypsies and those of mixed race and handicapped people exterminated.

Then I received a few horrible letters from my cousin who was interred in Kazakhstan. She told horrible stories about how hungry they were and how hard they had to work. Their father died after one year in a Siberia mining camp under horrible inhuman conditions. His son, then a medical student, was drafted into the Polish army and the Germans interred him and later he was freed.

It was turning nineteen forty-one and I finished my first year of university. At the beginning of June, we were supposed to return home for vacation.Now it is getting very bad. We found out through big newspaper headlines that the German people were destroying all the freedom of the people. There were all kinds of Russian propaganda.

I was still studying like crazy and I received a note from my father saying that he didn't want me to come home. Then my mother wrote to me that my father was not at home any more. I soon found out that my father had run away to the deep woods and he stayed there incognito with his farm friends for about two months. My mother would stay with him in the woods for a little while and then she would return home to check on the animals at home. She was such a good woman.

The Communists kept coming to our home all the time, asking her where my father was and she wouldn't tell them. She did tell them that he had gone to visit their children, and they would tell her to have him come to see them when he returned.

My father kept on hiding and he was very lucky that nobody killed him. They kept on mobilizing all the men they could find, because like the Russians before, to them, everyone was a spy. They arrested so many of our people.

Stupid me, I had to take an exam and it was one of my last exams. It was an exam about the History of Communism. Oh, it was a horrible exam! I remember that it was only about seven thirty in the morning and I was on my way to school and already bombs were dropping. War had already started between the Russians and the Germans.

When the Russian soldiers saw me, they made me go with them. They took me to a group of fifteen or so people, all men and women, no children, and I couldn't understand what they wanted with me. So I told the soldier, "Listen, I have my exams to take and I have to go back." He screamed at me, "You stay here!" They ordered us to go to a large cathedral that was nearby and it was surrounded by a fence. They ordered us to stand next to each other by the fence and then they held us there with their guns. I guess they thought we were spies, I don't know. I started to pray so hard, and guess what happened? The German planes started shooting over our heads at the Russians, and the Russians became so frightened that they ran away too.

I never went back to school. I went back to my landlady's and within a week many German soldiers arrived in Lviv. We started to run up the street. People were so happy to see the Germans that they were giving them flowers or whatever they had. We were in seventh heaven thinking, now we will be free. *Finally our Ukraine will be free!*

* * * * *

I forgot something that is very, very important. The leader of our church, Metropolit Andrey Sheptyckyj, in the West Ukraine, came from a very noble family. He was an extremely well-educated man and his superior was the pope in Rome. My father always told us that this man was a saint because of all the good things that he had done. His wealth, he divided among the poor and he always helped everyone that he could. His brother also was a monk in a monastery. When the Communists came, his third brother, who was a landlord outside of Lviv, they shot this brother and all of his family. Their land was confiscated by the state.

To our surprise, somehow they did not touch the metropolit because I think they were afraid of the world's opinion about what they had done. But, when the Communists returned to Ukraine in nineteen forty-five, they poisoned him and he died as a martyr for his church and his Ukraine. Unfortunately, it is a big puzzle to me that Rome did not make this lovely, giving man a saint.

In World War One, during the war between Russia and the Austrians, the Russians occupied West Ukraine. They arrested the metropolit, then the young bishop, and sent him to Siberia. After a few years, when Russia was undergoing their revolution, their Czar was killed and our bishop was released and he returned to our West Ukraine.

* * * * *

Now it is spring of nineteen forty-one and the war between the Germans and Russians is in full progress. I had never seen such beautiful uniforms or such handsome soldiers. They were tall, blond and very clean shaven. They were such elegant soldiers. They were all very polite and when they came to our street, I went to talk to them. My landlady was originally from Germany but she didn't want to go back during the Russian occupation because her husband was Ukrainian.

They asked me about my family and I told them where my father was. They told me that when my father comes home, if we need anything, they will be very happy to help me. Why would we not think that their coming was not a Godsend? We had been dealing with the foreign devils for so long that now we thought we had some good people.

Two or three days later, somebody came and knocked on our door. I opened it and I almost fainted. Two young German soldiers stood there. I couldn't believe my eyes. They were in their early twenties, so clean and so handsome. They brought me a letter from my father and they gave me some food from whatever my father was able to collect. And they told us that my father was very worried about me and my brother. They wanted news about our family because in a few hours, they were going back to that village. I wrote my father a letter and they took that letter back to him. My landlady, who was also German, was so happy that she found some vodka and she served them a drink.

After that my father sent somebody to bring us home and we had a beautiful vacation. My brother needed only one more year to graduate from high school and I still wanted to study medicine. We were so happy to be home even though home wasn't the same as before.

When the Germans arrived and were in control, they opened the jails. The jails were filled with dead bodies. Now I will tell you a story, you might not believe but it is the absolute truth. The Good Lord is my witness. I came from a big extended family and one of my cousins was a priest. In Ukraine if your cousin is older than you, we would call him "uncle." Before they left, the Communists were still taking people and killing them. They took my cousin in Lviv and put him in jail. They killed him and then hung him up. They slit his belly open and put a dead baby inside his belly. *The Good Lord is my witness that is the truth.* I'm ninety-one years old and whatever I tell you, that is the truth!

The Communists killed so many people; they piled one body on top of another. They mobilized everyone they could find. The soldiers would go to Ukrainian teachers and tell them, "You come with us!" If a teacher asked them where she was going, they would tell her, "This is only temporary and you will come back." They would take them and push them to get them where they wanted them to go.

Now I am once again at home and there are all kinds of German soldiers walking through our village, going east. And then a German general came to our home and he stayed with us because we had a big home and we all spoke German. My father began to question this general about how the war was going and what Hitler thought about everything. The general replied, "Ukraine will be free from the Black Sea to the North Sea and from Peremyshl in the west and as far as Russia in the east. Hitler will not occupy Ukraine.He wants Ukrainians to be his friends. He cannot control fifty million people" Hearing this, my father was in seventh heaven!

Our Ukrainian people were world famous for all kinds of needlework, cross stitching, artwork, and most especially the painting of our Ukrainian Easter eggs. Both my grandmother and my mother had made many and some of their artwork was given to this general. We still had some chickens on our land and some of them were killed so that my mother could cook some of her delicious food for our new friend, the general. Oh boy, we were so happy.

I spent all that summer at home and we felt quite safe, even though some had been killed in our village by the Russians. But we all breathed a sigh of relief. Maybe the Germans were our saviors after all.

Then we had a visit from our old landlord. They were all so happy too, because he told us that they were now going to go back to their old places and life would go on as before. The landlord told my father that because our old landlord speaks Ukrainian, and due to his German ancestry, the Germans have given him a big, big position in Lviv.

Then about a month later, I received a letter from my cousin Doris and her now husband, who was a lawyer, who had previously been in a Polish jail. My uncle's son-in-law and his daughter belonged to a Ukrainian organization and they formed an underground government to run the state in exile. They were president, vice-president, ministers etc. My uncle's son-in-law was supposed to be the Minister of Justice. They were all waiting for the Germans to arrive in Kiev because they were going to proclaim our Ukrainian independence. Upon hearing all this news, we were all so happy.

In the meantime they were in Lviv. Our organizers already had the nucleolus's statement and were ready to take over our state and run Ukraine. They were just waiting for Kiev because Kiev is the capitol of Ukraine and it is a large and very beautiful city. The Germans were still fighting and hadn't progressed as fast through West Ukraine as they had hoped. And our people were just waiting to see what would happen.

Then, you won't believe what happened! As we were all hoping and praying to be free of the Germans, the Gestapo came and arrested all of our newly elected leaders. They even arrested my cousin, who was already pregnant, because she was very politically involved. Once arrested the rest were all shipped to concentration camps in Dachau. We couldn't believe it because the German Army was already progressing through Ukraine to Kiev.

In the meantime, Kiev became free but nobody had declared our independence. Some Ukrainians who had run away, and other immigrants, all came back to our homeland and some were shot. My father was out of his mind and he couldn't believe what was happening. He kept saying over and over that he didn't believe it. There must have been a mistake was all he could say. He had started to buy more farm animals. After all, now Ukraine would be free.

The worst mistake that idiot Hitler made was not to make Ukraine independent. Instead, he made our country like a slave. Some of our leaders and the men and boys were arrested and sent off to concentration camps. My cousin Doris was again arrested and after sitting in their jail for a couple of weeks, they decided to let her go. They told her, "Lady, if you value your baby's life, don't play politics!" She took her belongings and came to our home because she knew that Lviv was not a safe place to hide.

She found out that her husband had been sent to a concentration camp, and my father could not believe it. He said, "You will see, next week the Germans will let them all go." But he was wrong; they were kept in prison until three years before the death of Hitler.

Now the German's drove through our country like they owned it and they laughed in our faces. Everyone began to have doubts and all those who had been under Russian control all those years, began to ask each other, "Who's better, the Russians or the Germans?"

Hitler divided Ukraine into a separate government, with the capitol in Kiev, which was just one or two miles from the Russian front.

After that, the army wanted to make Ukraine free and the stupid Gestapo and their stupid leader Hitler were afraid to set Ukrainians free. He set Slovakia free, but not us. One thing they did, the Germans were very, very organized. They put restrictions on the amount of food we could have. You could have only one egg per week. Everyone was treated the same. We were still hungry but we were not starving because we now had food stamps. We were only existing.

I was so glad to be home, but it was not a nice vacation. I was not really happy because so many of my friends were now dead. We were still at war, but we could still see each other and we could eat. My mother had once again planted a big garden and we could once again go to church without being afraid. We started to organize our lives as much as possible. It was still difficult because the Gestapo came to Lviv and they began to run things their way. And guess what happened? The Germans opened a medical school and a pharmacy and then they opened an engineering and a veterinary school, too. I was shocked!

There is no Ukraine anymore. Everything is now German. All of our Ukraine is now a part of Germany. They have annexed all of our country which made our people very, very unhappy. Then the Germans started to persecute us, and the Gestapo was horrible.

All the schools were in the German language. I applied to their medical school and to my great surprise, I was accepted. We found out that the Germans had selected some of our Ukrainian people, who had studied in Germany, to be teachers. They were also bringing some German professors to our country to teach. In Kiev, life was still horrible. The Russians were still in the underground killing people, and it was very bad. But in Lviv, at least it was clean.

Once I had been accepted at medical school, I realized that I didn't have many clothes to wear. So my mother once again found a seamstress and she came to our home. She made me some dresses from my grandmother's old suits.

My brother and I had been staying with this German lady but she could no longer keep us. My brother was ready to finish his last year of school. We were staying with my father's old professor and his wife. This professor was retired in Lviv. They were wonderful to us. My father had promised him that he would bring the professor all kinds of food from our farm.

At that time in Lviv, we had electric cars, and if I went to take one, I had to stay in the back. They told me that the front part was provided just for the Germans and their allies. If you were Ukrainian or Polish, you must step back. I couldn't believe it. If you went to the bathroom, there were also signs that read: For Germans Only. We could only use a public restroom that was a dirty, shitty place! In the regular grocery stores, the oranges, bananas, apples, and all the beautiful foods were for: "Germans only".

Well, our stupid politicians thought that if they were friendly to the Germans then they will make us independent and maybe Hitler will agree. But Hitler saw it differently, his way of thinking was: "We are the ruling class and you, Ukrainians, are our slaves. And you will see that when we win the war."

And thank God they didn't win, because Ukraine was so fertile that the Germans would bring their own big land owners into our villages and we Ukrainians would be working for them as their slaves. At that time, the Germans might allow the children to go the fifth or sixth grades but no college. Of course, all the Jews and Gypsies who had been to our homes and we considered our friends, were all sent to ghettoes and other special German places. One day a nice Jewish lady came to see my father. She was crying and when my father asked her what was wrong she said, "They are gathering all of us Jews and we are going to be sent to the Jewish ghettoes." My father asked her what "ghettoes" meant. He had no idea what was going to happen to all those poor, innocent people.

My poor cousin Doris was now ready to have her baby and she was hiding in our home in the village. My father told her that she needed to go to Lviv find a good doctor or a hospital. My father spoke to our landlord, who owned a truck, about Doris. He told him that she was due to have her baby very soon and the landlord took her to the hospital and she had her baby. After that she hid in her girlfriend's house for about two or three weeks until her baby was stronger. Then she came back to our home and she stayed with us until the Russians came again.

In the meantime after all that had happened, our young people had had enough of the Germans and they started to once again form our Ukrainian underground. They were fighting against the Communists and against the Germans, too. I couldn't understand why my people did this because they had never won against the Russians or against the Germans. They were not strong enough to have an army.

Now, my mother's brother went to a place away from Lviv where you could take special health treatments if you had illnesses. You could take a special shower there that would help you feel better. And they had some dirt that was radioactive and it was supposed to clean illnesses from the human body too. At that place, my uncle opened a high school for students who wanted to be teachers.

My uncle was then about fifty-four years old and there was a woman who he knew very well when he was in Stryj. She was a lawyer and was about thirty-five years old. They got married and in nineteen forty-two; she had a baby girl, Maria.

My brother was still in school and I had graduated from the gymnasium in nineteen forty and I was studying medicine in the German language because now I was in medical school. Since I was quite fluent in German, it wasn't so difficult for me.

The longer the Germans stayed in our place, Ukraine, the more the Gestapo came, and the war was getting stronger. I don't know what happened to the German soldiers. They were nice, clean gentlemen soldiers and suddenly they were all gone.

In the meantime, the Germans were going beyond Kiev. We were not waiting much anymore. We were all very unhappy with the German tactics and politics and we Ukrainians were very, very disappointed. Finally it was not so easy for the Germans to travel from the West Ukraine to East Ukraine. The further they were going east the worse the war became.

The outbreak of war started in the spring and now autumn was coming and it was getting cold. The further the Germans were from civilization, the harder it was for them to deliver food and ammunition because they were also becoming short of gasoline. They were so desperate for any kind of food to feed the soldiers, they were killing animals and anything else they could find to eat, but even that was not enough.

Once they came to Kiev, Hitler showed his true face. He was a butcher, a heartless, Godless man. Our people finally began to understand what kind of leader they were dealing with. Kiev had been longer under the Russian control than West Ukraine because they were only under

Russian dominance for two years. But in East and Central Ukraine they were under Russian rule almost seven hundred years. We in Ukraine had some interruptions from Russian rule, like in nineteen eighteen, we had three to four years of independence.

Well, it was easy to see that the Russians were not going to give up Ukraine territory as easy as the Germans had thought. The German politics were horrible; they had no sympathy, no feelings at all for Ukrainians. They treated Ukrainians, especially us in the East Ukraine, like we are their real slaves like some places in Africa. They were horrible!

In Kiev, the Russian Army left for the East, moving further away from Ukraine, and the Germans began killing the people like dogs. They called East Ukrainians Russian spies and they also killed many Jewish people. Some of our well-known writers and nationalistic people survived the Communist yoke but many were shot down and killed. That's the way it really was. My poor father was so bitterly disappointed.

Some Gestapo came to our village and took their food by force. They would go to all the villages and take all the livestock that they could. Perhaps because my parents knew the German language very well and because he was a priest, somehow they tolerated him that first year. But we could say that each month our living conditions were getting worse.

Winter was coming and my brother and I came home for Christmas. It was all right but not like before. We had some food for the table but it wasn't really like our old Christmas. We didn't have all the twelve traditional Christmas dishes, but we didn't complain. After all, we still had some food to eat. Doris and her baby were still staying in our house.

My father tried to get more cows and to organize our farm. Now we began to hear that the Germans are starting to need people. Why? Because their soldiers were dying and they had invaded so many other nations their manpower had been stretched very thin. They needed more farmers in Germany, and their ammunition factories needed more people. They had to force their old people to go to work for them. Now in their "genius", they finally realized that they could take their young slaves and put them to work for them for nothing.

The Germans went back to the villages with their big trucks and asked the young girls and boys, "Would you like to come and work for us in Germany?" And what did they have to lose? They had no jobs, no money, and for many, no place to live. The Germans gathered them up by the truckloads and took them back to Germany where they were given jobs in the munitions factories and on the farms. Later on we heard that some were very badly treated but some were not treated so badly after all. It just depended on which factories and which farms they were sent to.

Time was crawling by and the large cities in Germany, in general, were becoming ruins because the Americans and the English were starting to bomb them. For instance, Berlin was in a horrible state. Nuremberg, which used to be a very beautiful city, barely had any buildings left, as was evidenced after the war. Munchen and Hamburg, etc., were the same.

Now the young people from West Ukraine were not willing to go to Germany as requested and less and less would go. The Germans would come to the village selectmen and tell them that for a couple of days or a week, they will need a certain number of young men and women. The Germans would go back to the villages and take the young people by force. And the selectmen would have to help them or they too, would be shot.

Then the Germans became very smart. They would go to the towns where there was a high school and they would go to the principal and tell them that they would need students to work for them. They would take the older kids out of their classes and the Gestapo would come and select a certain number that they needed. The students were pushed into large military vehicles to be transported to the German factories, farms, or ammunition factories, or to help clean the ruins from the city streets. The boys or girls who were sent to help on the German farms, maybe they had a better life than being in the factories or cleaning the streets.

In the meantime, life was becoming very terrible; everything was becoming worse and worse. When we were in medical school, we were not afraid so much because we didn't think the Germans would do anything to us.

Now it is becoming Christmas. The first Christmas under German occupation was not too bad, but the second year, we started to feel really bad. We started to feel that the occupation was never going to end.

Somehow our medical school was still open and I was very surprised that they hadn't sent all of us medical students to a labor camp. We heard that the young people from East Ukraine were all treated very badly in labor camps in Germany. They all had to help make signs which read, "OST" which means "east". These signs indicated that they were not from the west.

We were still being segregated in Lviv. We were not allowed to use the German bathrooms. Boy, was everything horrible and we still didn't know how very terrible everything will be.

My cousin, Doris, whose husband had been sent to a concentration camp, was still getting a little note from her husband every once in a while saying that he was still alive. She and her little baby were in hiding and they stayed with my parents the two years that we were under German occupation. Of course my parents were very gracious and very good to them. Whenever I could go and see her, I was shocked to see how she had changed. She was very thin and seemed much older than she really was but she was always very good to me.

We started to hear from my father that the Ukrainians were starting to form a big Ukrainian underground. And hundreds and hundreds of Ukrainians were going to hide in the woods. Nearly all of the other invaded countries had their own underground forces. The Japanese and the Turks were German allies and they didn't have to worry. The Poles, Checzs, Ukrainians and Jews were the ones who really had to worry. We did have some Jews in our small villages and they were ordered to go to the bigger cities, to the ghettos.

Then in the spring of nineteen forty-three, somebody wrote us that the Gestapo had come to our house and they had taken all the food from my parents. They also took all the ingredients that my mother needed to make food with, like flour, salt, butter, oil, etc. My father begged them to leave. He told them that he had children and a family. They pushed him around and a soldier with a gun took him and tried to hit him. But another man stopped the soldier and he told my father, "You have grass and tree bark, make a soup and eat the grass!" My father was out of his mind with anger. That time was very hard.

67

The Germans did not allow the Ukrainians, who were still trying to farm, to bring food to the cities. The Germans issued us "food stamps" but we were not given enough stamps for even one day of food. If Ukrainian's dared to complain the soldiers would sneer at us and say, "You have stamps; our soldiers don't even have stamps. If you are still hungry, eat your stamps!"

All the villagers were so heavily taxed that they didn't know what to do. If they had kids in schools or relatives in cities that needed food; they had to hide it. Because if the Gestapo found any food items in your suitcases, they would drag you aside and you would be shot dead.

I didn't know who was worse, the Germans or Russians. If the Russians didn't shoot you right away, they would send you to Siberia. But the Germans were very, very bad. Unless you were a "real" German, a "Reichsdeutsch", who still lived in Germany", or a "Volksdeutch", those who had lived outside of Germany for many years but still felt allied with the German cause—these were treated very well.

My girlfriend came back from Germany and she told me that she wasn't on the German's side. I still felt that she was a "Reichsdeutsch" but I had nothing to do with her because she worked as a telephone operator in Lviv and I didn't see her too often. Her father was there in the village and then he disappeared and I don't know what happened to him. I lost touch with all those people.

My mother had a cousin who came from a poor, huge family in Ukraine. After World War One, this cousin, who was a young girl, came to the United States to live with her uncle. Later on, when she grew up, she married and went to live in New Jersey. She had two children with her husband and then later on, at age forty five, her husband died in a car accident. She had a son who was ten years older than her daughter and her daughter was five years younger them me. Her brother completed his schooling at the highly respected Massachusetts Institute of Technology in Boston. He was very smart in technology, and after his graduation, he was drafted into the Army where he trained as a pilot. Later on his plane was shot down and he was killed.

In the spring of nineteen thirty-nine, my cousin and her young daughter who lived in the United States, came to visit her dying mother. At first they stayed with her mother in the village and then they stayed with the brother in Lviv, with my aunt's brother.

When autumn came, they needed to return to the United States. In the meantime, war broke out and they had to stay in Ukraine and they could not return to the United States. They stayed a whole year and they endured the hunger and misery of the rest of us. Then one day, because at that time the Russians were still trying to remain friends with the United States, an American ambassador came to Lviv and he gave them a ticket. They went to Rumania by train and stayed in that war-torn country for two weeks. From Rumania, they went to Rome, Italy, and from Rome they went by boat to the United States. They were very nice people and she helped us very much when we were in Germany. When her son's plane was shot down and he died, that poor woman was left with her daughter Alice, who is my cousin. She is now eighty-five years old and I am still friends with her to this very day. She now lives in Florida and she is my neighbor.

It was autumn and very cold and the German Army was moving close to Moscow and Stalingrad. Now, the Americans of which I was not very happy, were openly helping the Russians. They were sending them food, planes, and I think even some soldiers. And if it hadn't been for them, the Russians would not have won the war.

Stalingrad was a horrifying place. We heard by radio and by others that hundreds of thousands of German soldiers were dying. It was difficult to think about all those human beings, young and old men, dying in horrific pain from bombs, bullets, and starvation. It was such a horrible distance away, and in East Europe and especially in the East Ukraine and Russia, the roads were no more. It was turning winter and it was unbelievably cold and there was no way to deliver food to them. They had no food, no oil, so why would they go to Stalingrad?—because Hitler wanted the shortest route south to find gasoline and oil. And they lost the war because there was no gasoline to deliver the soldier's food or ammunition. And they couldn't fly their planes either. Hitler was insane. Why didn't those generals or someone pull Hitler aside and stop to think about how many men were dying? Stop the war! Stop the front! Stop the insanity!

In the meantime, the African front was wide open. Rommel and Hitler were losing. Rommel wanted to stop the front there in Africa, and

Hitler called him back to Germany and told him to shoot himself. And Rommel killed himself. The Germans and Hitler were shrinking by the day. Then we heard that Stalingrad had fallen and the Germans were in full retreat. Whoever was left was lucky to still be alive and hundreds of soldiers were put in Russian prisons.

Life in Lviv was still very hard. The Germans were still being very vicious and we still were going to medical school. We would return to our home in the village and bring some hidden food, but really, we were starving. We were starving because my father was so afraid to bring us what little food he had.

Now it is spring but it was still very bad. I was in my second year and I was still taking my exams. For me, it was very important because I wanted to finish pre-clinics. We needed to follow the German rules in school. The Germans have two parts of medical school, pre-clinics was two and a half years of chemistry, biology, pathology and physiology, etc. You have to pass all your exams and then you go to the clinics where you would study human physiology and human diseases, etc. Medical school lasted about six years.

* * * * *

During the German occupation, I forgot to tell you many things about how mean and cruel the Germans were to us. In the next small town, maybe ten to fifteen miles from us, there was a very good, religious priest. He was a widower with six children. His name was Father Kowcz. One of his children, a daughter, was my age. I became acquainted with her when she came with her father to visit before the Germans came or before the Russian invasion. Her father was a very good man. When the Germans started to send the Jewish people to the ghettos and concentration camps, the old priest felt so sorry for them. He had a big parish house, very large and beautiful, and he hid these people in his house or in his church. Then one day, someone sent a notice to the Gestapo that the priest was hiding Jews, and the Gestapo came and arrested him and the others. Four or five months later, my father found out that this lovely priest had died in the concentration camp.

The second year of German occupation arrived and they were taking food right and left from all the farmers. They would go to the town or city hall and say they needed arbiters, zwangs, which were forced laborers, for a couple of days. It was not easy to find any laborers and nobody wanted to go with the Germans to work for them. The Gestapo wanted only the youngest, healthiest, and strongest people to work for them. They would go from door to door or to a local school to take the students right out of their classrooms. Most of the mothers never saw or heard from their children again. Sometimes, if the students were very lucky, they would be sent to help the German farmers and some of the farmers would feel sorry for them and give them food and try to help them.

I would like to point out that in every nation; there are good people and bad people. Some are very generous, others might be very stingy. Some might be very honest and others are nothing but crooks. When I was young, I never realized all this but now that I am growing old, I can easily see this for myself.

Another thing that I would like to point out is, I had a girlfriend in medical school and we studied together and we were very close. We would always go out together. She had a cousin who was a teacher in a small village. Her cousin was about thirty-five, married and had two small children.

Then came a horrible tragedy. One day someone killed a German soldier, but nobody knew how he died, by accident or by other means. Anyway, they found him dead and the Gestapo came to the village around two or three in the morning. They took about forty or fifty men and lined them up against a building. They counted every tenth man, took those ten men out of the lineup and then they shot them all. We were all shocked but the Gestapo did this all the time, it was nothing new. The poor wife was left with two very small children to care for.

* * * * *

In the meantime, my best girlfriend was moving out of Lviv because her parents didn't want her to stay there any longer. She moved to where they lived in the village. And I moved to live with my father's professor and his family. They were a lovely couple. They had a little room available. My brother was still waiting to graduate from high school and he had to stay in Lviv, so we moved to the old couple's home. About once a month, my father was able to bring us a little food and we still had the food stamps. We were never filled with food but we survived somehow.

That spring, both my parents were working in the fields and God probably felt sorry for us because everything was growing so beautifully and it was only May. The Germans hadn't confiscated that food because it was still growing in our fields.

In the meanwhile, Stalingrad fell and the German Army was retreating back to Kiev. Now we knew that the end for Hitler was coming soon; we just didn't know how or when. In my naivety, because I didn't know much about politics, my father thought that there would be a revolt in Germany. That they would kill Hitler and some democratic army would then come and take over and they would join the Americans and they would come. My father was a crazy optimist. There was one time that they tried to kill Hitler with a bomb and his arm and leg were injured but he was not killed.

Now we started to see all kinds of injured soldiers that we hadn't seen before. They were coming east from Kiev and Stalingrad because Lviv was still quite safe. Our medical school and the hospitals were so full of injured soldiers that they had no place for regular patients.

My brother had finished high school and the young men were all going into the underground. The Ukrainians were still at war fighting Germans, fighting Russians, always fighting.

My father wanted my brother to join the seminary to be a priest. He told him that he knew the director of the Catholic Theological Seminary and he could help him to get accepted, but my brother did not want to do that because nearly everyone on my mother's side was a priest. He looked at my father as if he were insane and told him that he was going to fight. He was not going to be a priest.

I was finishing my last exams because I thought that no matter what happens, I will at least have half of my studies finished. Some of the professors were still in their offices, and we would take our exams and they would grade them. I begged one professor to give me my exam early and he told me told me to come back in the fall, but I convinced him to give me my certificate early. I could see that he was very upset by my request, but he gave me the exam and I received very high marks.

Then I went back home and it was my very last day. The Russian front was moving like crazy. My father heard on the radio that the Russians were moving very swiftly toward our town, and the Germans were filling the world with how they were winning and it was all propaganda. One thing good I can say about the Germans was that they did not persecute my father like they had during the Russian occupation. He could still go to church and he held mass every day and they would still come to our home every second or third day to see what food items they could steal. Like us, they too, were very, very hungry.

I remember that my father said that the war situation was very grave. The Germans had already left Kiev and were moving towards West Ukraine. The Russians were pushing the Germans every which way; there was nobody left to fight them. I asked my father what we would do. We knew that we couldn't stay there and be controlled under the Russians. Stalin was still in power. My father didn't know what to say to me. I told him that I didn't want to go to Germany. He told me, "Maybe I will stay here, or maybe we will go to the Carpathian Mountains in the south." He gave me some food and kissed me and he told me his younger brother had a very good job. His brother was a forester/engineer in the southwest from Peremyshl, which was almost on the Polish/Slovakian border. My father told me to go there and maybe I could go to Slovakia because they were good to us. Slovakia was now independent and the Germans didn't bother them.

My father told me that if worse comes to worse and the front comes to Lviv, do not stay there because there will be terrible fighting and we don't know what will happen to us. If the front comes, the Germans may evacuate us; we didn't know what was going to happen.

Anyway, I went back to Lviv and I stayed with Professor Husak, my father's professor. When I got there, the professor told me, "Marusia, it is very bad, it looks like we will have a big fight here in Lviv. The Russians are pushing the Germans back and it looks like they will be here in a week or two. There is going to be a terrible battle." I could not believe what I was hearing! He said, "Why don't you pack your suitcase and while it is still quiet here, go to your uncle's. Maybe you will be safe there." So, I packed my suitcase, took my books, and went to the train station.

Peremyshl now belongs to Poland, but at that time, it still belonged to our Ukraine. I had to go to Dobromyl through Peremyshl, and with my luck I had to wait all day and finally there came a little, old, slow moving train. The trains were packed with people, but through sheer luck I pushed myself onto the train steps and boarded the train to go to Peremyshl. It was only going about ten miles per hour, but finally I arrived in Dobromyl.

My uncle lived about ten miles away from the train station and I had to walk. I didn't have time to write to my uncle that I was coming because there was no mail service, and my poor uncle almost dropped dead when he saw me. He thought there was a catastrophe at home or that my father had died.

I told him the latest news story about the German's retreat and he didn't believe it. He thought that the Germans were still fighting in Kiev. He couldn't believe that my father was frightened too.

At that time my uncle had three children, and then my uncle's friend came and told him that the situation was very grave and he said, "Let's pack our suitcases and take the horses and go somewhere south to the Carpathian Mountains."

My aunt started to scream that the Russians will never come here but my uncle was not so sure. "Slava," he told her, "maybe we should go to Slovakia."

Then we heard that the Russians were running wild through the countries. Maybe they will destroy our house. Maybe the Carpathian Mountains will be a much safer place to hide. So they decided to go.

Two or three days later, his friend came with covered wagons and his own family to my uncle's place. My aunt didn't want to go to the mountains. It would take many long days of traveling, but my uncle was adamant that we go. Then we started to pack everything that we could in the big wagon. I didn't know where my parents or my brother were. Finally we left and we were driving the horses. The kids were always crying. I think we were going south to the mountains, twenty to thirty miles a day.

The closer we got to the Slovakian mountains, the more we started to see Slovakian soldiers. The Germans had decided that they would try to stop the Russians in Lviv.

It took us three days and three nights to get to the Slovakian borders. I was the one who drove the horses because my uncle had a badly infected hand. And we had no medications or a doctor. I was afraid that he might get blood poisoning. I did all the jobs. The village didn't want us there so we stayed in the fields. We slept outside on the grass. On the second night, we heard shooting, screaming, crying and yelling coming from the village.

We heard shooting very close by; it was the Czech or Polish underground. Then they started to shoot at us too, so we hitched up the horses and left. Finally we got to the Slovakian mountains and the border. There were a couple of German and Slovakian soldiers stationed there and they demanded to see our papers. I had to show our passports and I lied to the soldiers that we are going to visit our family there; they let us go through.

Now we were finally in Slovakia, I thought I was in heaven, but we were so hungry, the children were so dirty. They brought us food and water and then they found a place for us to stay and they fed us. The Slovaks were wonderful to us and treated us very well.

The next day, my uncle met a priest and he said, "Maybe your brother is here, you never know," and the priest told him to go to the little village of Margetsany. So we went to Margetsany to the parish house, and guess who was there—my parents.

I learned that as soon as we had left my home, the front rolled in very fast, and as fast as they could, the people had to get out. The priest was a very nice elderly man; he had a nice parish house and a beautiful church.

My mother and my aunt cooked and cleaned, and my father started to help the old priest in his church. We stayed there two months. Then my father came to tell us that the Ukrainian underground was getting stronger and stronger.

My father was asked to be the assistant priest because the parish was Eastern Catholic who belonged, like us, to Rome. In that village the priest also found a place for my uncle to stay. It is coming to August, and the old priest told my father that there was a good medical school in Bratislava, the Capitol of Slovakia. After discussing this with my father, I wanted to go to Bratislava to continue my medical studies.

I couldn't believe it; everything was so quiet and tranquil in Margetsany. The village was very small with only four to five hundred people. But that paradise wasn't to last very long. We went to sleep that night and sometime in the night we heard very loud noises. The Russians had come to the priest's house. The end of paradise.

The Russians were already sending partisans to Slovakia by parachutes and they would go to the villages to search out everyone. We packed our suitcases and by four A.M. everything was finished.

My uncle, my father, and two other carriages went west to Slovakia. We went only ten or so miles and we were stopped. The German soldiers stopped us on the road and told us to go back to Preshov. That was in the east and so we went back and there were only German soldiers everywhere. Next we had to go to the train station and there were only animal cars and we were pushed into them. And the hell started.

Our suitcases I never saw again. We were packed like sardines into the animal cars, the doors were slid shut and they took us to Strashof. To me it was nothing but a labor camp. We stayed there about two months and that was the most miserable place I have ever lived in, in my life. There were bombings most every day or night.

When we got to Strashof, there were no young men to be seen, just old worn-out men. They watched us like hawks. Women and children were pushed into temporary shacks and we had to share the bunk beds. On arrival we were forced to wash with some kind of foul chemical to kill the lice or bugs. We couldn't sleep at all and we were covered with bed bugs, fleas, and bites and that was even worse than the terrible food.

The food was horrible and not enough to survive. Each morning and night, we had some black horrible coffee with a slice of dark bread with some margarine on it. In the noontime we had *einttopfgericht*, which was a very thin soup and with some microscopic pieces of meat, and it smelled horrible too. My father told us to: "Plug your nose and eat, because if you don't eat, you will die!"

A lot of the workers were sent to Strashof. I don't know why they called this place a "temporary camp" but it was true in a way. The workers didn't stay there longer than two or three months and then they would be sent to another labor camp. But while you were in Strashof, you worked very hard and the conditions were horrific.

My father had a friend, and somehow he found this friend with his wife and three children in a labor camp. He was a hard worker and he had his own company in Ukraine during the Polish occupation. This man had been an old bachelor and he had married very late in his life. His wife must have been at least twenty or thirty years younger than he and she was a beautiful lady. She was an older sister to one of my private teachers who had been very good to me. They had three small boys. At that time one of the boys must have been around eleven, another boy was about five, and their baby must have been about two or three months.

I don't remember exactly what they fed the labor camp workers but the food must have been horrible. Their youngest and next oldest children died and only the oldest boy survived.

One day I was standing outside by my place and a woman came by with a very small baby. She brought a few pieces of wood, and not very far from where I was standing, there was a hole in the ground. She put the wood into the hole and she started a small fire. From her clothing, she took out a small package of powdered milk and water. She poured the liquid into a cup and placed it on the fire to heat milk for her baby.

Nearby, there was a Gestapo prison guard who must have been at least seventy years old. And when he saw her light the fire and begin warming the baby's milk, he came over and with his foot, he kicked the wood out of the hole and destroyed the fire and her milk. The woman began to cry, telling him that her baby would starve. He didn't care about her or the baby; he turned and walked away.

It is now nineteen forty-four. We were there almost two months and our conditions were horrible and we were miserable. We were always so hungry and bitten by all the bedbugs. I was so thin that I could hardly walk and my father had developed a terrible cough. I was so afraid that he might get pneumonia. My father was so depressed because he couldn't believe that Hitler was still there. He kept telling me that soon

Hitler would be defeated. Father kept saying that Hitler's generals must have a few brains left and soon they would revolt because on all fronts everything was breaking down. Father kept looking for a revolt that never came. Father kept praying that the German soldiers would revolt and they would take down their horrible leader.

I kept hearing more and more that we had been held there too long and we were told that they were going to transport us west. Then I heard that there were three places for us to go. The best one was if we could go to the farms, because at least there we wouldn't starve. The second was a munitions factory which was not so good, but the third one was really horrible. It was a street-cleaning job in the cities of Hamburg or Berlin that had been bombed.

It is now the beginning of November and it is getting very cold. Of course in the camp where we were, there was no heat for us. Then they gave us some papers so that we could leave and told us we were going to Hamburg, the city on the water. And to our horror, my uncle and aunt and all the other Ukrainian people were going to be taken to Hamburg to clean the streets from the bombings. Hamburg was very far way.

Once again, we were packed like sardines into the dirty, filthy, stinking animal trains. It was nauseating just to get near the animal cars. The cars had very small windows that were high up at the top of the walls, and we were not allowed to open the windows. It was the journey to hell!

We never traveled in the daytime, only at night, because the Allies would try to bomb the train and the cities. We were just starting on the journey by train and my father told me that when he was an Austrian Army officer, he had visited Vienna a few times and it was a very beautiful city.

I was in one cattle car and my father and mother were in another. The German guards didn't want us to have anything and they stole everything from us. We traveled, and traveled and traveled and usually it was at night. The German Red Cross brought us some horrible, horrible soup. It seemed to take forever for us to get to that city; I think it took almost a week. It seemed that all my poor father could do was pray and pray for our safety. He never stopped praying.

Then we were getting close to Nuremberg. This once beautiful city was horribly bombed and as we got closer, we could hear the American planes and hear the bombs coming at us. We heard screaming and hollering but we could not get out and see what was happening because we were still under guard. This went on all day and into the night and then, we heard nothing. Suddenly, it was quiet, very, very quiet.

Finally, it was morning and it was very, very cold. Someone finally opened the doors of our cattle cars and we could see three or four wagons far away on the other side of the train station. We didn't know where in hell we were and the guards had all run away. We got outside and went to the very small station and then we saw what had happened. The whole front of the train and the railroad tracks had been blown up. We were free! But we still didn't know where the hell we were or even if we were alive or dead. We didn't know anything. I believe all this happened because of my father's many prayers.

There were about a hundred of us and we were walking around and five or six people came to see us. Some of the men were from the train station and one was a village priest. They looked at us like we came from Mars, asking us who we were and where did we come from. My father was always the spokesman for all of us and when he told them who we were and where we had come from, they couldn't believe it. Then they asked us if we were hungry and my father told them that we hadn't eaten for two or three days, of course we were hungry! They brought some carts and took us all to a large building that looked like a gymnasium or a school.

They gave us some food and they treated us very well. They called that little place Forchheim; it was a small town in Northern Bavaria. God was good to us and must have heard our prayers because we didn't have to go to clean the cities. Now, they didn't know what to do with us. They called us refugees. We were people from many places; we were not Germans, we were Ukrainian, Poles, and many others nationalities. We were all kinds of people from many eastern parts of Europe.

They brought us straw to sleep on. They didn't know what to do with us. My father begged them not to send us to Hamburg. Then the town manager came to meet us and he gave us the good news! He told all of us not to worry because they had a big paper factory very close to Nuremburg that we could work in. But he was lying; it was a munitions factory. And this was about six months before Hitler committed suicide in nineteen forty-four.

They gave us some hope, we didn't have to go to Hamburg after all; we were going to stay in Forchheim. We stayed there about two or three days and they were really quite humane. They gave us bread and brought apples to the children. The priest came several times to visit us.

They told my father not to worry because my father was our spokesman, and they told him that by the paper factory there were barracks for us to stay in. They didn't tell us this but these barracks had been built for prisoners of war—American soldiers. But when the Swiss Red Cross came in, they told them that the prisoners of war could not stay there. The Red Cross told them that the barracks were not suitable for human beings and they didn't allow any soldiers to be housed in those barracks and all the captured soldiers were sent to another place. Lucky us, that was where we were to go. It is now the beginning of November and already there is snow and it is very cold. These barracks had no running water and no heat, and we were just second class citizens.

Those barracks weren't good enough for the soldiers but they were good enough for us. Nobody cared about us. But I was surprised because those Germans from that small town seemed to be very humane. Why would they do that for us?

They brought all of us to those barracks and they told us that they would put ovens in the buildings for us for the winter. Each building was separated by a long corridor and the rooms were really only large enough for one person. Because there were so many of us, they would put a whole family in one room. In our small room was my father, my mother, a maid and me. We slept in bunk beds. My parents had the bottom bed and I had the top, while the maid made a bed on the top of a long table.

Then they told us, "Don't worry, you will be fed and starting tomorrow morning, you will have to work from six in the morning until six at night. The factory is going to feed you breakfast, lunch and supper." We couldn't cook in our room because there was nothing to cook on.

Then they brought us some small wood stoves and those stoves were nearly useless. You could warm up some small stuff and the women tried to fix food on these small stoves.

Right away they took us to the paper factory. On the first floor, it was a paper factory, but that was not where we were taken. We soon found out that the three other floors, which were underground, were for the munitions factory. To my surprise, there were no young men in the factories, only women and a few very, very old men. And all of the guards were also very, old men.

On our second day at the factory, we saw only very young, beautiful women. Every morning they were escorted to the munitions factory and at the end of the day, they were driven back to where they were staying. These young women did not work with us; they worked on a different floor. Finally when we got closer to them we saw that they had patches on their clothes that said, "OST Worker". They were under very strict control and they were mostly from East Ukraine, Belarus and Russia. My father felt so sorry for them and he tried to go and talk to them but they were not allowed to talk with us. One of the old guards told my father that the young women were taken to an old prison to sleep when they weren't working.

Now, the allied bombing was getting very bad. It was said that the Americans didn't bomb during the day but they were coming every night and I was so scared of the bombing. I told my father that I wanted to run away and he told me, "Honey, it doesn't matter where you are, in the building or outside the building. If they drop the bomb, you will be dead."

It was getting very, very cold; those heaters they gave us didn't help at all and we were freezing all the time. My teeth were getting bad because the food was so poor. I had so many cavities. I went to my supervisor and told her that I had a toothache. She gave me some powder but I told her that I needed to see a dentist. And she told me that there were no dentists. She told me that they didn't have dentist for "...you guys. They only have dentists for Germans. You are not allowed to go."

About a week later, I went back to see my supervisor because my teeth were still killing me. But she still wouldn't allow me to go. I had a few pairs of shoes when I got there but they were stolen from me. Now I needed some shoes because the ones I was wearing were full of holes. So I went to the supervisor again and she wrote me a paper and told me to, "Go to a shoe store and because you speak German very well, I'm sure they will give you shoes."

So a few days later, I was allowed to leave work a little early and I took the paper to the shoe store and gave it to the woman there. The lady looked at me and asked if I was German. When I told her that I am Ukrainian, she wouldn't sell me any shoes. So I had to go back to the barracks without new shoes. But then, somebody from "our people" gave me a pair.

It was Christmas again. It was the most horrible time that we ever had even when we were under the Communists. We cried for our homeland and we sang some songs at night and my father blessed a piece of bread because that was all we had.

I didn't hear anything from my brother, or from Doris and her child, or my mother's brother. I knew Doris' husband was in a concentration camp. We didn't hear from anybody.

After Christmas, somebody came to our people and told them that the Americans and the English were in France. My father wanted to know where they were and why the war was still going on. We still worked from six to six every day and that was our schedule seven days a week.

It was now about the end of February and we knew that Germany would be kaput any minute. We knew that the Russians had taken over all of Ukraine and we heard that Stalin was killing all Ukrainians right and left. And that our Ukrainian underground was shrinking every day. The killings are horrifying.

One day after work, at the beginning of March, we were at the bunker and in came two priests. They came to find my father and they said the factory will be closed in a few days. One priest said, "I want you and your family to come and stay with me. You pack what you have and tomorrow I will come with another priest to get you." They brought us apples, which was a miracle because we hadn't seen apples since we had left Ukraine.

That night we packed all that we had and we couldn't believe it, the very next day they came to get us. They took me, our maid and my parents to their beautiful home in a small village in the woods. The parish house was small but very nice and clean. This old priest lived in the downstairs, and upstairs there was a kitchenette, two small rooms and a small bathroom. Boy, were we happy there. The old priest's sister served wonderful, normal food for us, and we stayed in that wonderful home until the Americans came at the end of August.

My father was very worried about my brother Myron and my uncle Paul and he talked to the old priest about them. The priest told him that there were many dense woods here, and that he would try to help. So that priest talked to the other forester and my uncle got the job, and the other forester brought him to us. Now we had five other family members to worry about. The old priest, worried that the townspeople would learn of what he had done, offered to let them stay in his attic. I loved my uncle who was like my older brother.

We found out that the old priest had a radio and he would invite my father to go at night and listen to the news. It was a German radio station and of course, the reporters would never say how bad the war situation really was. But the old priest understood several languages and he told my father that Hitler was already within the borders of Berlin and the Americans had already liberated France. Then we finally heard the news that we had all been praying for, for so long—Hitler had committed suicide!—on April twenty-fifth, nineteen forty-five. I will never forget that date! He came out of his bunker, killed his dog, and then his wife, Ava Brown, and finally, he killed himself!

Then my father called his younger brother to ask him what they should do. We knew that we could not go back to Ukraine and then we heard horrific stories about our homeland, especially about West Ukraine. There was a tide of killings of our people like we had never seen before. The Russians annihilated our underground. If it hadn't been for the Americans, with their help and food, Russia would have crumbled. They would never have won the war because they were so very hated by all the other northern block countries like Finland, Estonia, Latvia and Poland. Nobody wanted anything to do with the Communists.

If it hadn't been for the Americans sending the Communists all their munitions, the Russians couldn't have made it to the outskirts of Berlin. Why did the Americans help them? Well, the Americans have always been very poor politicians. And secondly, the Americans knew that without Russian help, they could not destroy Hitler alone. And if they could not destroy Hitler, then eventually he would conquer Russia and it wouldn't be long before Hitler would come after the English and the Americans. The Hungarians, Italians, Turks and the Japanese were German allies.

My father said to all of us, "Be very careful because I don't know what is going to happen." I told my mother that I thought maybe we could go to my aunt in the United States, and my father told me that it wasn't going to be that easy. He said that if the Russians are already on the German borders maybe they would come here too. I asked him how that could be. Weren't the Americans already in Bavaria? My father looked at me and told me that maybe the Russians will take all the refugees with them back to Russian territory.

Then the old priest came to see my father to tell him that the Russians have come to all the villages and told the refugees to pack their suitcases because they are going back home. Well, that was just another big lie. All those beautiful girls that had worked in the munitions factory where we worked, they were packed up and sent to a Siberian concentration camp, and many died there. What did those poor girls ever do to anyone? We found out later on that over five hundred West Ukrainian girls who were in a Siberian concentration camp went on strike and the soldiers tried to stop them. The girls thought that the soldiers wouldn't shoot them but they were all shot dead. And every year there is still a memorial service for those five hundred poor West Ukrainian girls.

The old priest once again told my father that the village leader had told him to watch out because the Russian and American soldiers might come to the village and if they come here, you and your family will have to pack your things and go back with the Russians. Boy did this scare my father! He knew how very kind the old priest and his family had been to all of us and we might not see that kind of kindness again. The priest told us that he had a big shed in the woods and that he would take us there into the deep woods to stay.

So we packed what little we had and left our lovely friends. In the woods we found the large shed. As he was leaving, the old priest told my father that probably the Russians won't stay too long and that he would come to get us once they felt safe. We stayed there about three or four days. The Russians did come to the village and they only stayed one afternoon because the only ones left in the village were the forced laborers at the factories. All of the young people had already fled the village. The old priest came once again and took us back to his home.

It is now the summer of nineteen forty-five. So now my father told us that we needed to do something; we needed to organize our lives, and especially me, because I desperately wanted to go to medical school. Once again, the old priest helped us. He took me to Erlangen, a city close to Forchheim, maybe about forty miles from Nuremburg. Before I had left Ukraine my mother had made me a little sack that I wore around my neck. This sack contained my important documents. We went to Erlangen to a medical school, and a nice girl talked to me and the old Priest and told us that they planned to open the medical school in December.

My father told us that the old priest had been so wonderful to all of us and that he would not throw us out, but we needed to find some place of our own because we should not take advantage of him. My father was very resourceful because somewhere, somehow, he found some Ukrainian boys and they told him that in the east of Herzogenauroach, there was a huge American airport there. There were many American soldiers waiting there to return to the United States. Some came, some waited, but all would go sooner or later. And he also told my father that there were some Ukrainian/American soldiers who also worked there.

My father borrowed the priest's bicycle and he went there and found some men who spoke our language. My father went to the mayor of that town and the mayor rented us an apartment in one of his big houses. It was on the second floor with a huge kitchen and two small bedrooms and a bath.

We took the apartment and we thanked the old priest and we left. My uncle was still staying there in the village, because he had small children and he didn't know what to do with himself. His wife had an aunt in Canada and I think my father and the American soldiers helped him to get in touch with that aunt because later on we got a package from them. Our maid, Nastia, had an uncle's address that lived in America and she received a large package from him. She was the first to leave us and go to live in America.

It must have been the middle of July because we had strawberries and new vegetables. Now that we had moved to our new apartment, we started to breathe easier. The Ukrainian Americans from the airport came to my father to ask him to serve a mass. So my father would go to the small chapel and hold a mass for ten or fifteen people each week.

Those workers would bring us some food and that was the first time I ever tasted Coke, the American drink. I poured the Coke into a little wine glass and tasted it and I said, "Yuck!" It tasted horrible to me, and all the men had a good laugh. The Germans still didn't have much food; they still used food stamps.

I was preparing to return to school and I was certain that I would be accepted, but I didn't have many clothes. Somebody told my father that the nuns had a school for young girls and they would teach them how to sew. I went there and they told me to bring them some material and they would teach me how to make clothes.

So my father told me that in Erlangen there was a store that sold German uniforms. I went there and I bought some uniforms and some men's woolen socks. My mother tore the uniforms apart and washed and pressed them and I went back to the nuns and I made myself some clothes. Then my mother tore the stockings apart and made me some sweaters and vests. Now, I finally had something new to wear but I didn't like the uniform colors, so I bought some clothes dye and I dyed the new clothes many different colors. I was so happy with my new clothes and my knee stockings.

My father got some canned food and some white bread, and guess what else— American cigarettes too, and boy, did my father smoke! I told my father not to smoke so much. I still needed shoes and I found a cobbler and he told me to bring him some American cigarettes and he would make me some beautiful shoes. I took two or three packs of American cigarettes and he made me two pair of lace up shoes. They were burgundy suede and so beautiful!

Now, I had no hat. Those nuns were so smart. They told me to bring them a piece of material and they showed me how to make a hat. They took my leftover material and laid it out flat. Then they took an eating plate and placed it on the material and cut a large circle out of it. Next, they cut a slightly smaller circle out of the leftover material and they sewed the larger circle and the smaller circle together. Then they made a hole in the smaller circle so that it would fit on my head. The nuns told me to decorate my hat myself. Since I still had some pieces of different colored suede from my shoes, I sewed some flowers and leaves to my hat and now I had a beautiful hat too. I was so proud of myself!

Autumn was coming and I went to Erlangen quite a few times. If I ran into other students in that city, I tried to talk to them about medical school, but because I was not German, they wouldn't talk to me.

Then it came time to be enrolled in medical school and I thought I would be one of the first to be selected because I had been in a labor camp. I went to the school and the lady gave me all the necessary papers and I filled them all out. I took the papers back and gave them to the lady. She read through them and then she asked me if I was German. I told her no, I am Ukrainian. And because I was not German, I was not accepted. That woman gave me holy hell! She told me that there was no place for us foreigners. She told me to go back to Russia. She only had places for their own soldiers, soldiers who had spent their precious time defending their nation and they would get the first places. She was screaming and hollering at me and she was so nasty.

I went home and I was crying and crying. My father couldn't believe what I said. In my eyes my father was a genius. He told me that we needed to find an American Ambassador. My father told me that in Nuremburg there might not be an ambassador because that city had been completely destroyed. He wanted the ambassador to understand how we poor refugees were really being treated by the Germans. My father said that Erlangen was now the best city because they had all kinds of universities that hadn't been destroyed.

We went to the American Embassy the next day, and my father, who was dressed like a priest, asked the young lady for an appointment with the Ambassador. While we were telling the secretary what had happened to me at the medical school, the door opened and a handsome, young man came into the room, and my father told him through the secretary what we needed. That young Ambassador started to yell at the young secretary in English. I couldn't understand why he was so angry with her. I thought that probably he was angry because she was wasting her time talking to such low people like us. Then she said to us, "Do you know why our Ambassador is so angry? It is because of you! He is so angry that the German girl treated you so poorly! He told me to call that girl up and tell her that you should be one of the first to be accepted at that medical school. He is going to write her a letter and if you aren't one of the first to be accepted, he will fire her!"

Right away my father took me back to the medical school and that girl was like a different person. She was so sorry for having treated me so poorly. She kept repeating that she was so sorry and that she hadn't meant any of the terrible things she had said to me. And I was one of the first foreigners to be accepted to medical school! There was one other girl who was also accepted, and I could tell that she had been in a concentration camp because her hair had been shaved off and the Germans always cut off their prisoner's hair.

Now that I had been accepted, they allowed all my studies in Ukraine, but I had to go and study physics. I found a professor to help me, and after about three weeks, I passed the physics exam with a B+ and I was accepted in the clinics. I started the clinics and I was very surprised by all the professors because I'm sure some of them had been Nazi's during Hitler's reign. They were all very nice to me even as I was a foreigner. Perhaps there were about thirty or forty displaced Ukrainians studying in that medical school.

They started to form a Displaced Person's UNRRA, and this was for all the refugees who had been displaced and had no place to stay. These were people mostly from East Europe that had been involved in the war. They formed in many large cities and they were located in army barracks or in old schools that had closed.

In Erlangen there was a large place for us Ukrainians. There must have been about two hundred people and some from that place would go to the university to study. And some of the displaced people would go to work in Belgium in the mining places. Some wrote letters to their relatives in Canada, the United States, Argentina, Brazil, Australia, France, Belgium and England, and if they were lucky, in six months or a year they would be transported to those places.

My uncle was very lucky because he stayed in one of the displaced person's camps, and in a few years he went to Toronto to his wife's uncle's. And he was very happy there.

The professors were very, very good to me. I was a very good student and I spoke German fluently. I had no problems, but the other students were very cold and didn't want anything to do with me. I'll never forget that one day when I came to the class we had to change the rooms to study one subject or another. When I got there, the room was already occupied and there was just one seat that was still empty. When I went to sit down, the guy who was sitting next to the empty seat told me that the seat was already taken. When I told him that I wanted to sit down, he looked at me and said, "My friend is coming." Guess what? I stood up the full hour for the whole class. I'm sure there was no such friend; he just didn't want to let me sit there. Socially, the Germans could and would not tolerate us.

When the Americans came, we still had to have stamps just like in war time. We were still only allowed only so many eggs a week and it was very difficult to find fresh bread. My father was very, very smart in every way and somehow he found a butcher who had some fresh horse meat. To buy horsemeat you didn't need to have stamps. If you have enough money, you could even buy a quarter of a horse. When I saw the horse meat, I told my mother that I wasn't going to eat that because I loved horses. My mother couldn't believe me and she scolded me. "You eat pork and you know that pigs are some of the dirtiest animals on earth!" My mother made us some horse stew and guess what? It wasn't so different from very dry beef, but it was sweet. I was not crazy about it but if you are hungry, you will eat it.

I had always admired the Germans because they were always so disciplined. They were hard, hard working people. Even though they had lost the war, Hitler was now dead and I met some Germans and I couldn't believe it. Even though they had been through so much, they acted like nothing had happened. They continued about their business without a complaint. The German students were never lazy and they studied very, very hard.

In nineteen forty-seven, they started to talk about *veherung*, which meant "changing the money." This means that all the old money will be obsolete. Germany was now getting huge financial support from the United States, and overnight, Germany and its businesses became like the United States. All of the once closed, empty stores were now full of food, clothes, shoes, meat, etc. Any foods you wanted and could pay for, you could find.

My father now was working as a priest with the displaced Ukrainians and he would have a mass every Sunday at ten o'clock. He was still planning to go to the United States. In the meantime, Nastia, our girl, got in touch with her uncle and he was so happy she was still alive. Then we started to get packages at least once a month. We got chocolates and I'd exchange those for clothing and food.

The first package we received from Nastia's uncle had some stockings—nylon stockings! I couldn't believe it! During the Polish occupation, I was still a student and at that time, students attending a Catholic school were not allowed to have nylon stockings. So I only wore those nylon stockings during the summer time and I was so careful with them because I only had one pair.

Then we had a big blow and we were very depressed. We found out that all those geniuses that we called the "big brass", Stalin, Roosevelt, and Churchill, had gathered in Yalta and they had made some horrible, horrible decisions. All those idiot leaders of the United States, France, Germany, England, and Russia divided Central and East Europe. Then they gave a large part of Europe to that dog Stalin. Boy was "Dirty Stalin" happy! Now he could kill anyone that he wanted to. The West Ukrainians were still suffering and all the priests who did not want to become Russian Orthodox Priests had been sent to Siberia or exterminated.

My father was so afraid to write letters to his family, his sister and brother who were still in Ukraine. We heard through the grapevine that the worst persecution was in West Ukraine. Hundreds of priests and nuns who had been sent to Siberia had been exterminated.

Our Ukrainian underground was still in existence, but the force was dying out because the Russians were killing any they could find like rats. Later on I found out that my best girlfriend had married a classmate from medical school and they joined the underground and stayed in the Carpathian Mountains Underground Hospital. One day the Russians found out about their secret hideout and they threw a hand grenade into the hospital and all of those poor people burned to death.

When my father heard of this news, he was so depressed and he kept asking, "Why? Why? Why?" Why couldn't President Roosevelt and Churchill see what kind of a man Stalin really was? All these countries of Belarus, Estonia, Latvia, Czechoslovakia, Hungary, Poland, Lithuania and East Germany had been divided up, and of all the people that Stalin persecuted, the worst were the Ukrainians and especially our West Ukrainians. Stalin didn't care about the people or what he did to their lives; he gave the allies what they wanted.

Then about two years later, we learned that my beautiful brother Myron had been killed. He was only about nineteen years old and now he was gone. When my mother heard the news that my brother was dead, she cried for the rest of her life, literally, until the day she died. Her life was destroyed along with his.

Later on I went to visit my parents and while we were eating our dinner, I told my mother that I was going to go back to my room early because I was going to a dance. Boy, did I get hell about that! She was so upset because they had just found out that my brother had been killed and she couldn't believe that I would go out to dance when my brother had just been killed. She went to tell my father that I "had no heart." And I got big hell that time, I can tell you that.

Then we learned that Doris' brother was in the Ukrainian underground, and he was trying to get other soldiers to cross the Slovakian borders and he was killed too.

Later on we got news that Doris was in Munich and also that my mother's brother and his wife and child were in Vienna. The Communists had taken them because at that time, the eastern part of Vienna was controlled by the Russians. My uncle and aunt were waiting to be taken to Russia.

Lucky for them, my uncle contracted typhoid fever and he was very sick. The Russians were very scared about that disease because they didn't want their soldiers to catch it. So they put him in a German hospital in Vienna. One of the doctors felt sorry for my aunt, and she begged him to take her child Maria to a safe place. And my aunt stayed with her sick husband in the hospital and that saved them from going to the concentration camp in Siberia.

Somehow, probably through Doris and her husband, my aunt, my uncle and Maria were smuggled to the western part of Vienna and they were all saved. After that they all went to Munich where there were many Ukrainians.

I was still in medical school in Erlangen and I studying like a fool and what little money we had was running out. The only money we had was because my father would get a few dollars because we were refugees. Now we found out that there will be an International Refugee Camp for people like us in Erlangen, and eventually all the people like us would immigrate to other countries. It was called UNRRA (like the Red Cross), and my father found out that there were some Ukrainians there. The UNRRA would give them food, room and board, and they could go to school there for free until they were placed somewhere else.

Somebody told my father that we should go, and my poor father was so scared that one day the Russians would come. He was afraid because the Americans were so ignorant about the Russians and their treatment of Ukrainians, and that the Russians might come one day and take us back to Russia.

In the meantime, my father decided that he would go to look for a room and board in Erlangen to be closer to me. In those days, because of my huge medical school and all of its students and many refugees, it was very difficult to find a place to live. My father was walking around the streets and a man asked him what he wanted. My father told him he was a priest and then he told him about me. This man was very nice and he had a home that had a little room, a bathroom and a kitchenette on the outskirts of Erlangen. My father was so happy and he moved to Erlangen too. There was no longer an airport in Herzogenauroach because the Americans had closed their airport and the soldiers had returned to the United States. When the Americans left, they left a lot of their things behind, and I was lucky to get a typewriter and lots of paper and these things helped me with my medical studies.

Erlangen was a very friendly city for foreigners and they had all kinds of schools. So my father became a priest for the Ukrainian students. Many refugee students came there to study all kinds of subjects, subjects like economics, law, ministry, history, and pharmacy. There were all kinds of subjects for us to study.

Very near where my father had found us a home, there was a Roman Catholic Church and my father went to see the priest who lived there. The priest told him that he could have a mass downstairs in the cellar, and every Sunday he would hold a mass for twenty of more students.

My poor father had no income except for some packages that came from UNRRA for the refugees. And once in a while somebody would give him a few marks to hold a mass if somebody was sick or some relative had died. Then my father would go the refugee camp and have a talk with them, and somehow we survived. I was so glad that my parents now lived near me because even though we didn't have much food, my mother would cook for us.

The new landlord had a small garden and sometimes he would give us some vegetables and some rabbits. If I had some free time, I sometimes took an electric trolley and I would go to visit my father and mother.

I lived very close to the medical school and I stayed with an old maid who had a very nice apartment, and she was very kind to me. She had a few little rooms and I lived with her there. I found another Ukrainian girlfriend who had just been released from a concentration camp, and she still had very short hair because the Germans always shaved the female's hair off. She was Ukrainian like me. She was also a very good student, and was five or six years older than me.

In the meantime, I received a letter from my old girlfriend that I had been very close to in Ukraine where we had attended medical school. She wrote me a letter and she was now in the south of Munich with her boyfriend and she lived on a small farm. She begged me to help her come to Erlangen. Because her sister had already finished pharmacy school, she didn't need to study any longer. So her sister's boyfriend, her boyfriend, and my friend came to Erlangen. Because of my good heart, they all applied to medical school and were all accepted, but she didn't like to study medicine, she wanted to be a dentist. All three finished their studies and graduated.

I needed clothes very badly. I still had a few old things but nothing to wear if I wanted to dress up and I didn't know what to do. Nastia was now ready to go to America and she told me not to worry and that even if she had to borrow the money, she would send me some clothes. And true to her word, as soon as she got to the United States, she sent me some beautiful dresses, suits and coats. The Germans were already dressing up, but the refugees had nothing at all except the very clothes they wore on their backs.

My Baby Picture

My Paternal "Tanczak" Grandparents

**My Father,
Basil Tanczak,
an Austrian Soldier**

**My Father's
Theology Graduation**

**My Father's
Gymnasium Graduation**

Cisyk Family and Me

My Grandmother, Joanne Cisyk

My Aunt and Brother, Myron

My Mother with Friends

Father's Gymnasium Class - 1913

Ukrainian Wheat Harvest

Uncle Tolko - Died in WWII

**Helen Cisyk,
My Mother**

Rev. Basil Tanczak, My Father

Me and My Brother, Myron

My Brother, Myron, and Me

My Brother, Myron

Me at Age Ten

My Father and Me, Hala and Myron

Sernyky Parish House

**Me and My Parents
with Nastia**

Janczyn Parish House, W. Ukraine - 1939

**My High School
Graduation
1938**

Gymnasium Graduation - 1938

Myron's High School
Graduation

My Father, Age 36

Cousin Maria

Me, My Mother and Cousin

Ukrainian Football Team

My Darling George:

Because the Ukrainian always stuck together, finally all the Ukrainian students got together and opened our own Ukrainian Medical Association in Erlangen, of which I belonged. Stupid me and my big mouth, I told them that I had a typewriter, and to have a typewriter at that time and in that place, was a very big deal. As a student we always were writing papers and our thesis, and the typewriter helped so much. One day a very nice gentleman, who I knew as a fellow medical student, and who was a couple of years ahead of me, came to see me. He already had a Bachelor's Degree in Economics from Ukraine and he had finished his studies after the Communists came.

He came up to me and said, "Maria, I am George Dycio. Did you say that you have a typewriter?"

"Yes I do." I replied.

"Well, can I borrow it from you?"

"No," I told him. "That typewriter is not for you, it is for me." And not getting what he wanted, he went away.

And then one day, my old landlady told me that I had a guest, and it was George. He said that he needed to borrow my typewriter for one or two days. He explained that his writing was so horrible that he really needed a typewriter. I asked him if he knew how to type and he said that he would type his papers with just one finger. I told him that I was very sorry but that I needed the typewriter for myself. Well he finally left and he was not happy.

Two days passed and then somebody knocked on my door and it

was George again to beg me for the typewriter. After a couple more visits, I finally capitulated. I told him he could borrow it for only two days because I needed it, too. And he had no typing paper either, so I told him to go buy some paper. He looked at me and said, "Maria, I have no money to buy paper!" Well, he borrowed my typewriter and I gave him some paper, and perhaps a week or two passed and I never saw that typewriter again until I married him!

I think that his conscience bothered him because one day he came to visit me and I asked him where my typewriter was. He told me that he was not finished and that he had come to take me to the movies. I did not say anything more about the typewriter because I loved movies. We saw a movie that night. George was living in the holding camps for the refugees that the Germans called *auslander*, or foreigners, and he was commuting to Erlangen. He was living in that camp with his sister, her husband and her two children, and they helped him as much as they could.

Then he found a nice room with a lady who didn't have any children, and she liked him so much that she always called him her son. Every once in a while this landlady gave him some food but it wasn't often.

Then somewhere I heard that there was going to be a medical dance and four of us Ukrainian girls, all students, decided to go to the dance. The war was now over and though we couldn't dress like all the American girls, we were all dressed up in the nicest clothes that we had and we wanted to have a good time. How ignorant can you be? We went to the dance and we sat in the corner like four dummies. Nobody asked us to dance. Nobody spoke to us. I was sick and tired of sitting with those girls and I was so very disappointed that I cried.

Then I noticed a lady physician who worked at our hospital, so I went to sit with her and she told me to go dance with her husband. I think I danced with her husband a few times and then we got out of there. My girlfriends agreed that that would be the last time we would ever go to those idiotic places. If you went to those places and you didn't have a boyfriend, you didn't get asked to dance.

When I saw George again, I told him off because he still had my typewriter and he didn't ask me to the dance. He looked at me and then he said, "Maria, how can I go to a dance? All I have are these lousy, old clothes. I have no suit, how can I go there?" His clothes were very clean but in bad condition.

Our friendship was becoming closer and closer and then one day George came to see me. He was so happy. It was as though somebody had given him a million dollars. George, though still a student, was an excellent, excellent hockey player. "Maria, guess what! I have been accepted into the International Hockey Club and we played with the American Army players." He played with them two or three times and then he said, "Guess what? My friend and I have been asked to join the American soldiers' hockey team and they are going to pay us." To play for pay! That was the first time I had ever heard about playing for pay.

At first I thought that that would be good for them, and I asked him about his studies and his medical career. He said that he would have to drop out, and I scolded him about dropping out of medical school. And that's how stupid some men are because he told me that when he plays for the Americans, he will be very rich. He thought he would be richer than any doctor. At that time he was more interested in playing hockey than studying medicine.

When I told my father about George's plans to leave his medical studies to play hockey, my father could not believe that George would do such a thing. My father told me that if George would do that, then he was not the man for me. My father felt that if George was really that smart, he would never leave his studies to play that "idiotic" sport. My father told me that George was no good for me and that I should say goodbye to him and find another man.

Then one day George came to see me and showed me some money. He told me that he was going to go buy himself a suit, new shoes, and everything else a man needed. He offered to give some of his money to me, and I told him that I didn't want any but if he wanted to buy me some chocolates, that would be fine.

About a week later, he came back to see me and he was dressed so beautifully. He had on a new coat, a hat and shoes and all of his clothes matched right down to his shoes. He was dressed like a king. He had even bought himself a new attaché case. I asked him how medical school was going and he told me to forget it. So I told him that if he was forgetting about medical school, I was going to forget about him. I didn't want a "dummy hockey player" for a husband. When I told him that I wouldn't go out with him if he quit medical school, he took off and I didn't see him again for a couple of weeks.

Then one of his friends came to see me and told me that George was in the hospital and he was very sick. George and his friend had not yet been accepted into the American soldiers' hockey team; they had just had "try outs." I asked what is wrong with him, and I was told that he had been hit in the head with a hockey stick so hard that he had a cerebral concussion. He was in the hospital for nearly a month, and he had severe headaches for several years after that. When I told this news to my father, he was glad and said that maybe now George would get his brains together and he would stay in medical school.

When George was finally released from the hospital, I asked him if he was going to continue to play hockey. He looked at me and said, "Are you crazy? They don't play hockey like we do here in Europe." I looked at him and said, "Didn't my father try to tell you that you would be without your head, hands and hair?" He looked at me and he agreed that hockey was not for him. So, George returned to finish his medical school studies.

It was nearing the time for us to finish medical school, and I could not understand one thing about medical school in Germany. Germans are very precise people and very well organized, but the way they ran the school, I didn't like it at all. The first two and a half years you have to study everything. They don't care if you have already studied a certain subject. They felt that you have to have so many hours of practice and then you must take some exams called, "pre-clinics". Then when you pass those exams, which I had already passed in Ukraine, you go into "clinics" which is usually three years or sometimes it is even four years of study. After you finish all the clinics, and you have all of your papers filled out, and if everything coincides with their rules and regulations of the medical school, then you are eligible to take the "Exams". The Exams were comprised of forty-two to forty-four exams.

These exams are horrible and usually more than half of the students failed. I think the medical schools do the exams like that on purpose because they have so many medical students. And by scheduling such extensive exams, they can weed out the academically poorer students. Those exams were horrible to say the least. I had forty-two subjects, and for some, I had only one day in between. Thank God that I was one of those students who studied all the time, but some students didn't study like I did.

Internal Medicine was five subjects and we had to take each exam separately. Pathology alone was dissecting parts of dead bodies. We had a microscope exam, a written exam and an oral exam. All of these exams were with four different professors. I want you to understand how very difficult all the exams were. Then we had general surgery, orthopedic surgery, neurosurgery and thoracic surgery. And we had both written and oral exams with different professors. To take your exams, you must have a minimum of three to four people to take the exam.

I had one boy friend and two girl friends that I liked to study with, and one of these girl friends had only taken about half of her exams and she was already exhausted. My mother told me to invite her for dinner and then we could rest in our house and we could go back to study. I told my friend Ulana she should come with me to my home for dinner. She told me no. She said that she was going to stay in her room because she was too tired. So I went home and had dinner with my parents and then I returned to my room to study.

When I went back to my room, she was not there, and then I found her letter. She said that she was tired out and she cannot take studying any longer. She said that she was going to her mother's in Munich and she was not coming back. She had a boyfriend in Munich who was ten or twelve years older than she and she married him. Within a month, she, her husband, her mother and her brother all left for the United States. I thought it was very foolish of her after having gone through all of medical school and all those exams. It was very stupid of her to have left. So I wrote her a letter to say come back and return to medical school, but she didn't want to. Years later I met her somewhere in the United States and she already had two children. She was then working as a medical technician and they didn't have much money. She very much regretted not having finished her medical studies.

I was in the middle of my exams and I had finished Internal Medicine. Then I had to take my pharmacology exams which took me at least two or three days to refresh my studying. Pharmacology was always a very difficult subject for me because there was so much math involved. I did not have time to finish, so I went to a friend who was a physician and got a letter saying I had acute gastritis. You couldn't not show up, you must go to the school. I told the secretary all the symptoms I had and asked for a postponement. But I got no help. She told me that if I wasn't dead already, then I must go to take my exams!

You won't believe it but I failed miserably, and my professor wanted to give me an "F." I was in a state of shock because I usually got all "A's" and I just could not pass that exam. I told him that I was so tired and sick, "Please don't give me an "F"," and I started to cry. Well, he felt sorry for me. So that professor said he would take care of everything. He went to that stupid secretary and everything was fine. I went home and I had a whole month to study, and even though I earned an "A", he gave me a "B+" because of the circumstances.

George finished all of his exams and became a physician. In Germany if you pass all of your exams, you are not a "doctor", you are a "physician". You have to study for a Ph.D., to be called a doctor. George told me that he would study for his Ph.D., and he wanted me to do that too. I agreed with him because I thought that the title of doctor would be more prestigious and help you in your career. Since George had finished his medical studies before me, he then asked me to marry him. My father was not happy because I still didn't have my physician's studies completed. He gave me hell and he told me that unless I had that paper stating I had my diploma, he would not allow me to marry.

Through sheer luck, when I had first been in medical school, I had met a neurological professor and I found out that he had just come from studying neurology in the United States. I went to him and explained what I needed and he was the one to help me get a doctor's degree. I had written my thesis on "Nonne Froin's Syndrome in Spinal Fluid" and I had to find ten patients with this syndrome. After you have finished writing your thesis and take three separate exams, if you pass those, then you must defend your thesis before a panel of doctors. If you pass that, then you can have a doctor's degree. I was very glad to finish that and in February of nineteen fifty, I finally got my Ph.D. Degree.

My father wanted to go with the Roman Catholic Mission because they would allow you to go to the United States, provided you had somebody to sponsor you. The Roman Catholic Mission would not agree to sponsor him or give him a job. He was still a priest and working with the students.

Now that I had finally finished my studies, I had decided to get married. I felt that George was a good man. He was still playing hockey with his club and I attended every game that I could. I did not understand one damn thing about hockey; I only went to look at all the people and how they were dressed. Sports had never interested me that much, but I went to please George.

In the meantime, Doris and her husband and son were in Munich. I went to visit them and their little boy of about six. They had a nanny too. And I also visited my uncle and aunt at a refugee camp in Munich. He opened a gymnasium there for the Ukrainians. He and his wife had a little room there with their little girl, Maria.

My poor aunt Eugenia had no good clothes and I felt sorry for her. We borrowed a sewing machine, and my aunt and I sewed clothes for my aunt and Maria for a whole week. I was so happy to help sew them some nice clothes.

Doris said to me that she didn't think she would go to the United States after all because soon Ukraine would be free and it wouldn't be so far to go. Later on she decided to go to the United States as a guest of the Ukrainian Woman's Association of America and she stayed in New York. She had a big-shot friend there and they sponsored her visit. She bought a few new dresses with a few dollars and then she came back to Munich. He husband was very disappointed that Doris hadn't stayed in the United States.

I had finished my medical studies and George still played hockey from time to time. Then he found a job in Ingolstadt and he was given a room in a beautiful home. It was the home for the "big" Nazi's and the official headquarters for UNRRA. Nearby they had a clinic, and this was where my George worked. They didn't pay him much and sometimes he only received food for his services, but it was something.

My father was very, very worried because several of his nieces and nephews had been sent to Siberia. He was very afraid to write to them because he had heard how very horrible the persecutions were. My father just wanted to know where his family members were and if they were still alive. But he didn't dare to write to them because Stalin would destroy any of those who stood against him. My father found a distant cousin in Poland and through him, he finally found some connection to his family.

My father's youngest brother, Paul, was like my older brother. He, his wife and five children were very lucky because his wife had an uncle in Toronto, and they sponsored him to go Canada. My aunt was an excellent housewife for my uncle and their children.

My father was always worried about his sister and brother but he didn't know where she was. He always worried that the Communists had killed her. After being widowed very young, she had remarried.

Somebody, perhaps an old general, decided to gather a group of young men and bring them to England to participate in talks with the English brass. It was decided to take the young men to the Carpathian Mountains to show support of the Ukrainian underground. They sent fifty or more, maybe even one hundred of them, and the English dropped them by parachute into the Carpathian Mountains. Somehow the Communists already knew about them and the Russians shot them all. My father was so distraught. He was crying for days. That was so horrible.

MARRIED: October 21, 1949

George and I married. We had no money, but George's sister Ivanka and her family who had immigrated to Toronto in nineteen forty-eight because her husband had relatives there, sent me a wedding present. She sent me some clothing, some chocolate, and five dollars. That was my wedding present. George never parted with that money until we came to the United States.

The wedding was very small with only about twenty people. My uncle came with his wife and Maria, along with Doris, her husband and their son. George's and my best friends that we had gone to medical school with, all came too.

The wedding was in the church and it was very pretty and some of my classmates came to the reception. We had some hors d'oeuvres, pot roast and red cabbage. George was an excellent cook and he went to a bakery and he and my mother made some cakes. We had three or four beautiful cakes.

I didn't wear a white dress because I had no money. Maybe I could have rented a dress but I didn't know what to do. My old friend Nastia sent me a package and in the package there was a lovely dress. The dress material was very light, and in October it was already cold. She sent me a light gray coat and some beautiful blue material. I had a seamstress sew me a very lovely dress and I bought a beautiful pair of shoes. George bought me a lovely bouquet of roses and gave me a ring; it was a very simple band, but it was gold. We didn't have anything inscribed in the ring because we didn't have the money to pay for it.

We had a record player and we danced and danced until twelve o'clock. And my father had a very good friend who was German who became a Ukrainian missionary, and he and my father recited at my wedding.

The Honeymoon: I could not go back to my old apartment and my little room. George's landlady and her husband came to our wedding, and after our ceremony she came to us said, "Since you don't have any place to go, and you are now married, you can go to George's room." So for our honeymoon, I went to stay in George's room. It was a nice, beautiful room and I stayed there for quite a while.

In the spring of nineteen fifty, my parents left for the United States, I finished my doctor's degree and got a little job for displaced persons where George worked. I had very little money but it was better than nothing. At least we had a beautiful place to live and we stayed there all summer.

There were many Ukrainian settlements in the United States because before World War One and after World War One, many of our Ukrainian people were allowed to immigrate to the United States. Nearly everyone we knew had some relatives in America.

My mother wrote me many letters from the United States, and they finally ended up in New Brunswick, New Jersey, where they were living in a cellar. Some of my father's parishioners gave my mother a job in a big leather handbag factory. She had to use glue to hold the leather together to make the handbags. In just one year, she lost all of her nails and she suffered so much. She was in pain all the time and she was always getting abscesses in her fingers. But she stayed in that factory nearly three years until she finally found another job in a factory that made medical vials.

My mother didn't want my father to work in a factory, and he was trying to organize a religious parish. My father was trying to find some Ukrainian Catholics and he finally found about ten of them. Finally, they managed to save a little money and they found a better rent. It was in downtown New Brunswick and that place was very nice and it was across the street from a beautiful park.

Now they felt much better and now my father tried to find a place to hold a mass. Somebody told him about an old Italian priest. My father went to see him and he told the old priest that he wanted hold a mass. But the old man refused to allow my father to hold a mass in his church. So my father started to talk to a very old Methodist priest and the old man allowed him to go to his church. So after agreeing to pay the old man a few dollars, my father was allowed to hold a mass.

Traveling to the USA:

Finally we had decided to go to the United States, and we gathered my papers from the Catholic Action Group and Olesia's mother. And it didn't take us very long before we were ready leave for the United States. We traveled by train to Hamburg and we stayed two or three weeks in a camp. Then we were packed on army boats, ships that were returning to the states to be destroyed. We were two or three weeks on that ship, and everyone was so nice to us but the weather was horrible. I got so sick of meatballs and spaghetti and everyone was vomiting. George too, was vomiting and was so seasick.

Mamma Mia! We finally arrived in New Orleans and it was horrible because they were in the beginning of a hurricane. And I tell you that was horrible and horrible traveling. I think we traveled about four weeks. Finally we arrived in New York City. When I opened my eyes,

I couldn't believe such huge buildings! I saw the Statue of Liberty and when we got off the boat, we all knelt and kissed the ground! This was the twenty-first of October. Everyone started to cry and we all thought that we had arrived in paradise. The only gifts we got from our sponsors to the United States were some doughnuts and a lousy cup of coffee.

Now the UNRRA ladies or social workers tried to find a place for everyone. If the new arrivals did not plan to stay in New York and had to travel to another state, these ladies would help them to be sure that they would get on the right trains or find a place to stay. If the new arrivals couldn't speak English, there were translators to help them. They were very, very helpful.

I was so impressed with New York City. I had never in my whole life seen such tall buildings. George's two sisters were both there when we arrived in and they looked to us like such fine ladies. They were all dressed up and they spoke (to our way of thinking) English fluently. They were very gracious and lovely ladies and they treated us so well. George was the baby of the family and they were so good to us. Paula said to me that Maria's apartment was horrible and that hers was a little better. We took a taxi and they even paid for us and she even talked to the taxi driver in English. And to me, her English was very beautiful. *Note:* Paula will soon be one hundred and two years old and still lives with her daughter in Washington, D.C.

As we drove further into the downtown, I saw that the city was really changing. As a huge city, it was horrible, horrible to me. Everything was filthy dirty. To my eyes, it was nothing but a slum. I was so disappointed and disgusted by all the filth that we saw. The huge city's streets were smelly and dirty and littered with all kinds of things that people had just thrown there.

And I need to mention that even though Germany had just been through a horrific ordeal with the Second World War, you could still eat off their streets. Even though the Germans may have been poor, the Germans were clean, and maybe their houses were old, but they were always painted and repaired. The Germans didn't know anything but how to work. And everything was clean and lovely and in order. And once the war was over and Hitler was no longer, the Germans put all their bad memories aside and began a new life in the land that they loved.

Now we are in the wonderful, wonderful United States of America that everybody had always dreamed of. I thought that everything was free in America, the land of goodness. Ever since I was little, I would ask my mother if I could have some money to buy chocolates from a little store near our home. Or I would complain that I hadn't eaten any candy for a whole week. My mother would look at me and say, "What? Do you think we live in America?" As a child, I thought that everything was free in America and if you really wanted something, it just dropped in your lap as though you were a king. After all, America was the land of goodness, to all of us foreigners anyway.

When we finally arrived in New York, we were exhausted from all our weeks of travel on the sea. We had spent nearly a month on a crowded, old boat and my muscles were weak and I hurt all over. I couldn't wait to finally put my feet on dry land once again.

Finally we arrived at Paula's apartment, and to my horror her apartment was on the fourth floor and we had to walk up four flights of stairs. All of the apartments were connected by an outside corridor. Once you finally got up to the fourth floor, even the bathrooms were in the outside corridor. Their apartment was clean but it reminded me of the labor camps. And once in the kitchen, there was a living room and dining room together. And there was a small windowless room with a bed in it for the children and a larger bedroom for Paula and her husband.

We were eating in the kitchen and I asked her where she washed and Paula told me that they had to wash in the kitchen sink. They didn't have a shower and if you want to take a bath, you had to remove the kitchen table top and there was a bathtub under the table. I was very surprised by all this but I didn't say anything.

George's brother-in-law, Walter, had already finished his Bachelor's Degree in Business in Ukraine and he had a part-time job washing dishes in Howard's Restaurant. Paula had a degree in teaching and she told me that she was very lucky to be cleaning offices on Fifth Avenue from six at night till six in the morning. They paid her by the hour, she was very happy to have that.

Around six o'clock her husband and her two children arrived home and Paula made us such good food. She made one chicken dish that tasted delicious to me. It had boiled potatoes, chicken and string beans in it, and boy was that good! We had some cookies for dessert.

Then Walter told us that we had to see a much better part of New York and we went to see Broadway, and boy was that something! I saw all the huge advertising signs and the Camel cigarette sign with the camel smoking. As we were being driven around in the bus, Walter turned to me and said, "See Maria, all the rich people go to the theaters here in New York City and they have different shows all the time."

We called my parents to tell them that we had arrived safely. We stayed in Paula's home for about three or four days and we also visited George's other sister Maria's home in another run-down part of the city. They had only one child, a girl of about six. They only had a two-room apartment with a small kitchen, and it was located in a horrible section of the huge city. Maria was also cleaning offices with Paula, but her husband had been very lucky. He found a job with a Catholic store that shipped all kinds of Catholic items to other states where there were a lot of Catholics.

We were anxious to get to my parents' home, so we packed our things to go to my parents in New Jersey. George's brother-in-law gave us some money to take the train to go to New Brunswick. At that time my parents had been living in the United States for over a year, and even though my mother didn't complain in her letters very much about her job, I knew that it was horrible by what she didn't say. I had told her that as soon as I got to the states, I would find a big job for myself in a fine hospital. I would earn excellent, excellent pay and she wouldn't have to work any longer. Boy was I stupid and I had a lot to learn about the very fine United States.

I was very surprised at how clean New Jersey was as compared to New York, and my parents had a very nice apartment. The building had two floors and it was very clean and it even had two bathrooms. There was an old Irish lady and her old-maid daughter who lived on the second floor. They were pleasant and very nice to us.

My father started to be happy in his new country and he had started to organize a Ukrainian Catholic Parish, but he still had no place to go to hold a mass. He was surprised to learn that there were many Ukrainian farmers in the New Jersey area who had come to the United States before World War One. The old Italian priest had told him that he could have a mass in his church but it was for him alone. He did not want others coming to his church.

So my father asked the old landlady if he could hold a mass in one of the rooms in her building, and she said he could. But after a month or so, so many people were coming to mass, she told my father that he had to find someplace else.

After resting for a few days at my parents, George told me that we had to go and apply at the hospitals for jobs. I decided that we must try to find a medical position, but my mother did not want us to go too far away. She thought that we should try to stay in New Brunswick. I didn't want to work in New York either but we had to accept whatever position we could find. I promised her that we would visit her as often as we could.

George had written two or three applications and I couldn't believe it—he was accepted to the Bayonne General Hospital in Bayonne, New Jersey. I, too, had applied at many different places and to my surprise; all of my applications were declined at every place. Bayonne Hospital did not feel that a husband and wife should work in the same place. To my surprise and disbelief I could not believe that women doctors could be treated like second class citizens in the United States. I think I must have filled out at least twenty job applications at the medical facilities, everywhere we could think of.

George received a notice from Bayonne Hospital to go for an interview and because we couldn't speak English, he couldn't understand the letter. My father asked one parishioner who spoke English very well to come help us. He came and read the letter to us. He told George that the hospital is accepting him but they still want to see him in person. George didn't know what to do because he couldn't speak very much English.

The man told George, "I will go with you, and when we will talk, I will look at you and you just smile and say one word, "'Yes.' I will speak for you." Well, he went with George but they wouldn't allow the second person to go in with him. So that poor man was kept waiting in the waiting room. Poor George did like the man had told him. He smiled and said, "Yes. Yes. Yes." He did not know if he had gotten the job or not. He told the man that he didn't understand one word at all. But that man was very clever and he told George, "Never mind, in a couple of days, I will pretend that I am you and I will call to see if you have the job." Well, he was lucky once again because George was to start on

Monday, and he got fifty dollars a month. George packed his bags and left for his new position.

I cried and was very upset. Nobody wanted Dr. Mary Dycio, Magnum-Laude, with a doctor's degree, a Ph.D. even. I was very upset. Now I was so discouraged and upset. My mother was barely making a living and my father wasn't working.

We didn't have a telephone so I couldn't talk to my George. Finally one Sunday, my husband came home and I was so happy to see him. He said that it was horrible for him because he couldn't speak English. He had much writing to do with the patient's history and he needed to tell them what was wrong. He was on a rotating internship basis and after a year or two of training he could open a family practice. He was considered an "intern" even though he had a "physician's" credentials. He hated it. He was so nervous, tired and upset.

I was still waiting for a hospital opening but I could not even get an interview. I was so upset. I had even written to hospitals as far away as Albany, New York. But nobody wanted me and I was so discouraged.

I met a Ukrainian woman who worked in a dress factory and she told me that I should stop waiting for a medical position and that I should go to a factory and gets a little job there. She told me that I should go to the factory, and maybe later on a job would come to me in the medical field.

She took me to a huge factory where they made woman's clothing. It was nothing but a huge "sweat shop". It was the beginning of November and there was no air conditioning. She told me that the big boss could speak a little Slovakian and she told me that I should tell the boss that I was a seamstress. The boss came to talk with me and he told me that he wanted to see how well I could sew. He took me to a monstrous electric sewing machine. I had never seen one like that one before. In Germany all that they had were the old fashioned foot-treadle machines. I could sew on an old fashioned machine but not one like that.

The big boss gave me some material, and when I pushed the button to turn the machine on, the material got caught under the needle and turned over and over. I broke the needle and I thought I had broken the machine too. The boss began to scream at me, and I knew I wouldn't get a job there. But that woman began to speak for me and he hired me.

121

He gave me a job that had nothing to do with the sewing of the clothing, and I was paid fifty cents per hour. I had to prepare the clothing for shipping. I had to zip, fold, and button them, and one day the big boss came to see me. He told me that I had to work faster because everyone was waiting for me. So in a week or two, I became the perfect employee and I did my job very well.

Then one day, after I had been working at the sewing factory, we had a little coffee break and one of the women asked me what I had done in Germany. When I told them that I had just trained as a physician in Germany, they didn't believe me because a person who was really a trained physician certainly wouldn't be working in a clothing factory.

Now I was earning a little money, I felt better. I could see that my mother's fingers were so sore and swollen and she wouldn't be able to keep working much longer. She was so ashamed that her fingernails were gone; she always wore gloves to go out or to church.

It was November of nineteen-fifty. One day, we had about ten dollars and I thought I was a very rich woman. We went to the food store and we bought all the items that the three of us needed for a whole week. We paid nine dollars and fifty cents. We could not carry all that food to our home so we needed to take a taxi, and it cost us twenty-five cents and I gave the driver a twenty-five cent tip.

I had been working about a month in that factory and I was told that I could go to the high school because they had a night school for immigrants. And I wouldn't have to pay even one penny. So every day after work, from six until nine, I would go to that school because I had figured out that if I did not know English, I would never leave that factory. I would be a packing lady for the rest of my life. Boy did I study, and in one year I had learned enough English so that I could get by. Now I could speak seven languages. I had studied Latin for seven years, and if you know Latin, there is so much in English that connects to Latin and that really helped me a lot, especially in the medical field.

George was complaining less about his job because he was becoming used to it. I thought that now that I knew a little bit more English, I should try again to get a job in a hospital. But nothing. Then someone told me about a Ukrainian man who worked at the Squibb Pharmaceutical Company and that he had a doctor's degree from Germany. He had been working at Squibb for two or three years as a lab technician. He met my father, and my father told him that I was a doctor and that I was working in a clothing factory and that I was miserable. Finally, after about seven months of working in that clothing factory, I went to work as a lab technician's aide. And when I told them I was a doctor, they thought I was crazy. One guy told me that I should go to Newark, New Jersey because they have a hospital for infectious diseases there. So I decided to apply at that hospital.

The hospital was on the outskirts of Newark, and you had to be a genius to be able to know how to get to that place. The hospital was huge and beautiful, with maybe ten floors, and it was surrounded by a beautiful garden. I was introduced to the hospital administrator and he introduced me to doctor who was the hospital director. And then all the medical assistants came to see me like I was the "Queen of Sheba". Two of the doctors had been in the Korean Conflict, and all of the nurses and everybody else was so nice to me. They were so happy to have me. I finally had a job in a real hospital. This was the summer of nineteen fifty-one.

Then they showed me the real hospital, and it was a horror of horrors. Both the office where I had been interviewed and the doctors' stations were gorgeous, but not the rest of it. The floors were filled with people who were very sick or dying. One huge floor with about fifty beds was filled with women tuberculosis patients and encephalitis patients. The next floor was full of men who had tuberculosis, encephalitis and syphilis. Then other floors were filled with kids and young people who had succumbed to the extremely infectious polio disease. Sick and dying children with horrible diseases like measles, scarlet fever, and whooping cough filled other floors.

When I returned home later that day, for the first time in my life, as much as I wanted and needed a job, whenever I thought about that place, I was scared to my roots. There was no vaccination at that time for polio, and young people and kids were dying every day. There were two types of polio. The bulbar type caused many of those infected to die, but if they recovered they had no leftover side effects. The other type of polio was paralytic and it was also very terrible because it lasted a lifetime.

I didn't know what to do. Should I go to work there or not? The place was so disease ridden that I might contract a life threatening disease too and I was too young to die. My husband talked to me about all the things I was so worried about. And he told me that maybe it was best for me to stay with Squibb and maybe with my medical background, they would elevate me to a better position.

I can say that I was treated very nice, and all of the doctors had a wonderful dining area. They served us excellent food, and you couldn't ask for better treatment. They had the very best cooks and waitresses and there were four full-time doctors including me. They really needed many more doctors than we had and later on I found out that one of those doctors had never finished medical school. There was only one doctor who was "board certified", and I couldn't understand why he stayed at that hospital.

At that time, I still had not taken my "state boards" or anything because I did not have my internship completed. Now, I started to work. You had to start at seven for breakfast, and at eight A.M. we had a meeting with the medical director to discuss special cases and even the causes of death. We had deaths every day because it was over a thousand-bed hospital. I learned more practical medicine in that year than I had ever learned in my life. Boy did I learn—because there was nobody to help you. There was no one to ask for advice although I did call my husband once in a while. You were all alone and you had to make all the decisions about the treatment, should the patient go to the rocking beds or be placed on a respirator. These were all your decisions and yours alone.

I had to care for the encephalitis patients, perform spinal taps and I learned that I was an expert. I did very well, and to tell you the truth, the German medical schools were very good in theory but they didn't teach you practical medicine or practice this kind of medicine. To me, the American medical schools were very well-equipped and the staff was well-trained in hands-on medicine.

Every morning, I would get out of bed and the first thing I would do was to check my neck to see if it was becoming rigid. I was mostly afraid of contracting polio because it was in nineteen-fifties that the United States had a huge Polio Epidemic. We had a lovely twenty-two-year-old nurse and she came down with polio and that poor girl, in three days she was dead.

Maybe when I first arrived, I didn't give those doctors very much credit for all their hard work, but after I was there a short while, I could easily see that I had misjudged them. They worked like dogs, day in and day out. We had to take night calls too. This was considered a normal part of the job, and I now was getting two hundred dollars a month. They all treated me very nicely; they didn't push me around.

About once a month, George and I met on the New York subway, and because we were more familiar with the city, we would walk around to look at the buildings and city sites. Sometimes I would buy something for myself to dress up because my wardrobe was very small. On the Sundays that I had off, I learned how to go to New Brunswick and I visited my parents every third weekend. I would share my money with George and every once in a while, I would give some money to my parents. We couldn't afford to go to the fancy restaurants but we would eat at all the little outside kiosks.

At the end of that year, George told me that his hospital had asked him to stay with them and he didn't want to leave. So George started his second year at the hospital. We saw some of his family from time to time.

My uncle on my father's side was lucky because he got in touch with his wife's aunt in Toronto and they sponsored them. He and his wife and five kids all moved to Canada. And because he was a forester engineer, he got a very good job there. But he was not really so smart because he smoked too much and he died of lung cancer at age sixty-one, in nineteen sixty-nine.

My uncle on my mother's side, who was about sixty-five, wrote to us a crying letter asking what he should do. They had one child, Maria, and they were still living in that refugee camp in Munich and the place was going to be liquidated. My uncle had been a principal in a school but now the school was closing. My aunt was a lawyer in Ukraine and that woman was brilliant.

My uncle and his family got immigration papers to come to the United States. My father with his good heart helped them to get papers and they came to New Brunswick. At that time I was still working in the clothing factory. They came to our home and stayed one or two nights, and then our landlady told us that she could not have them all there. She told us to find them another place. Well, now that was a big problem. They had no money, how do we find them a place?

My father told my aunt that maybe she should try to get a job at the hospital. Because my father was a priest, he knew all kinds of people and he knew the nuns at the local hospital. So she was hired by the nuns as their cleaning woman, and she stayed a cleaning lady all the days of her life. After about a month, my uncle also got a cleaning job. About two or three weeks later, my father found them a small place, but they had to share the bathroom with others. Their little daughter, Maria, went to school, and even though she didn't know one word of English, about a year later, she was the top student in that school.

George told me that when he finished his second year, he wanted to be an Obstetrician & Gynecological Specialist. So he started applying to other hospitals, and I told him to tell them wherever he applied, that he had a wife who was a physician. I wanted to have a job where he worked.

Finally, we found one place where they would take both of us at the same time. It was at Mercy Hospital in Canton, Ohio. And they were connected with the Western Reserve Hospital. We were so happy because the Western Reserve Hospital was a very excellent hospital. And they had all kinds of residencies available.

I went home to tell my mother the good news about us leaving for Ohio. My mother was very upset about our leaving because she did not want us to leave New Jersey. Right away, she looked at the map and then she knew how far away it really was. She always believed that I would have a position in New Jersey. She did not realize that I was working in a hospital that cared for infectious diseased patients.

I was so happy, and George told me not to worry so much about my mother. We had to go by train to Canton, Ohio. It was a prosperous town because next to that town there were the large cities of Cleveland and Akron, Ohio. And there were many very large metal factories where they manufactured cars and tires. I was shocked to learn of the many Ukrainian settlements in that area.

We took our suitcases and went to the hospital and that hospital was run by nuns. A nun came to greet us and she was very nice. She asked me if George was my husband. She told us that they were expecting three married couples and by nightfall they would have a place for us. She told us that the Mother Superior had had a place emptied and the house was very close to the hospital. The hospital was very clean and they gave us a tour. I was very impressed with the nuns and the cleanliness of the hospital.

That night the Head Nun took George and me to the house they had prepared for us. That house had been abandoned, so what did the smart nuns do? Well, the downstairs on the first floor, they made into a clinic. The second floor was for us physicians. Each couple had one very small room and a bathroom. The only telephone was located out in the corridor, and there were three doctors on call all the time. That darn telephone rang all night long, and you never knew if the call was for you or not. Oh, it drove everyone crazy.

Now summer was coming and you couldn't open the windows because the outside ground was a parking lot and it was not paved. So every time a vehicle drove into the lot, our house was filled with dust and dirt.

Anyway, we were lucky that we got the jobs and we knew that we wouldn't stay there forever. George took a residency in obstetrics and gynecology studies for three years. I wanted to take my internship for one year and then study pediatrics, and George reminded me that they didn't offer pediatrics. But I wanted to work with children. I thought I would love that.

So I had to go to Cleveland to study. I started my internship with internal medicine, and most of those other doctors were very nice to me. I didn't care for the surgical doctors because they had such egos and they were always a pain in the neck. I also found out that there were many Germans there due to the large German colony in that area.

The only ones who were mean to me were the residents. You were really under their supervision. Some were so mean or lazy that they would scream and holler and demand that I write the patient's history for them. I was so tired and worn out. One even told me, "Mary, we can scream and yell at you and you have to say, 'Yes sir'." I didn't want to tell George of all my troubles so I told my father and he was wild. He told me, "Mary, that guy is not your superior or your boss! You go and complain to your superior about that lazy jerk!" I didn't want to do that but finally I was so tired that I had to. I went in tears to the big boss and he called that lazy man and told him off. Then I had no more trouble.

I had taken only one year of internship and I was not finished and I was now working in the operating room. There was huge excitement in the hospital because a female doctor had arrived from South America. She had come to take her surgical internship at our hospital. She was not bad looking and she was very outspoken. To me, her English was excellent and she was very confident in herself and very, very self-assured. We were told that we must be scrubbed and in the operating room at six thirty every morning that we were scheduled for duty. The residents and interns would already be there, all scrubbed and waiting to cut. In the operating room, delays were not allowed. The operations must always start on time, with no exceptions. Once the "gods" had arrived, we must all be prepared to help them.

On one particular morning, I was scrubbing with a doctor who was Irish or English, and he was a very nasty man and he was a real "God". I didn't like him at all, but in the end he was nice to me. He looked at the head nurse and demanded to know where the new lady doctor was. The nurse told him that she didn't know. Our hospital had about ten operating rooms so we thought that she might have gone to the wrong room by mistake. They looked and looked but they couldn't find her.

Now it was nine o'clock and she finally arrived. The surgeon took one look at her and he began to scream at her, asking where she had been and why she hadn't come on time. "Haven't you been told that you have to be here at six?" He asked her. She gave him a long look of disdain and she told him, "I was too tired! I'm not working for you!" Well, that was all that this "God" needed to hear. He replied, "Lady, pack your suitcase and leave!" And he fired her. The reason I have written this is to show that unless you were dead, you must be in the operating room on time, every day. There were no excuses.

My George was doing his obstetrics and gynecology residency, and I had finished my rotating internship and now I had to do surgery. Surgery was difficult because I had to learn how to cut. In those days, there was no Social Security, no Medicare; you had to have money in order to go to the hospital. We did have a clinic for poor people, and the patients would come, and even though we hadn't completed our studies, we had to treat those patients for nothing. Usually, because they had waited so long before seeking treatment, they were very, very sick people.

Then I went to obstetrics to train, and one day they called me and they wanted to know where the physician was. I told them that I didn't know, and with my bad luck, they called me to deliver a baby. I had never made a delivery before and the baby's head had already "crowned." Upon seeing the bulging birth membranes, I picked up a knife and the nurse grabbed my hand and she asked me why I had grabbed a knife. If she hadn't stopped me, I might have cut the baby's scalp. Thank God in Heaven that she stopped me!

One other day, I had more bad luck. I was called to the delivery room and the doctor still hadn't arrived. The patient was in the process of delivering a premature baby. She was a big, fat woman and by the time I got there, the baby and the placenta had been delivered. The baby and my gloves were so slippery that I dropped the baby and the placenta on the floor! But I really was lucky that time because there was nothing wrong with the baby. I didn't like obstetrics or gynecology.

Then I went to the Anesthesia Department for my rotating internship never dreaming that my specialty would become Anesthesiology. Dr. Frick had come to the United States from Switzerland and he was a very well-educated man who was Chief of the Anesthesiology Department at Mercy Hospital. He was in charge of that department and he helped me so much. He let me do everything. If I told him that I didn't know how to do something, he'd look at me and tell me not to worry because he was always by my side. I loved that department!

About a month later, he took me aside and I only had about one month to go to finish my internship. He asked me what I was planning for my future work. I told him that I must go to Cleveland, Ohio to the Western Reserve to begin my pediatric residency. Upon hearing that, he said, "Why do you want a pediatrics residency? I have a residency here in anesthesiology and after two years, then you could go and take further training in pediatrics if you still wanted to. Why do you want to go into pediatrics when you are so excellent in anesthesia? Do you realize what you are doing? First of all, you will have to deal with those pain-in-the-neck mothers and you will have office calls in the morning, noon and night. You may even have to get a part-time job because pediatrics doesn't pay that well. You are excellent and you really should study anesthesia; it is a beautiful field for a woman. You have very beautiful hands and your hands are made for anesthesiology."

I went home and when I told George what Dr. Frick had said to me, George agreed with him. My husband told me, "Mary, Dr. Frick wouldn't have offered you the position if he didn't believe in you. You have to believe in yourself." George thought that I could have a very good job and earn some good money there too. George still had about one year left in his obstetrics and gynecology studies. So, I went back the next day and I accepted. I loved that doctor and I was so glad that I made that decision. Dr. Frick was so good to me; not only was he my boss, he was my mentor and my friend.

The only bad thing about staying in the hospital was that I had to live in that awful, boiling room. There was no air conditioning and we still couldn't open our windows and I hated that place. But there was one good thing about staying in that hospital, it was kept very clean and we always had nice, clean sheets for our bed.

So I accepted the offer of Dr. Frick's Anesthesiology Residency for two years, and after that I would finish my specialty in anesthesia and I would become a specialist in anesthesia. They offered me one hundred dollars a month.

During my anesthesia residency, every once in a while I would find some money in my pocket. Sometimes it was a twenty dollar bill and another time it might be a fifty dollar bill, and I always knew who had put it there. Dr. Frick would look at me and say, "Mary, Easter is coming. Go buy yourself a new hat and some new gloves or something you need. Remember Mary, always wear gloves; a lady won't go to church without gloves and a hat." He always gave me money.

Now that first year, I never saw such a good and smart man. He was from Switzerland and he had a very beautiful wife and they had no children. They would invite the residents and other physicians, Dr. Shaeen, and Dr. Shirak, to their home. Dr. Reno, an anesthesiologist was always sick with severe eczema on his hands. He could not scrub his hands and his hands were in pitiful condition. I always helped him if I could.

Dr. Frick was trained in Belleview Hospital in New York, under Dr. Rovenstein who was supposed to be one of the first, most famous anesthesiologists. There were none before World War One. There were so many wounded soldiers and terrible injuries that really needed our help. World War Two was when anesthesiology became a specialty. As you can see, anesthesiology is really a very new specialty.

Dr. Frick liked me better than everyone else. As I said before, he liked me. His wife was an excellent cook. Supper was always so wonderful. There also was a Ukrainian family with three kids that we used to visit and we loved them very much. They invited us to their home and she would make all kinds of delicious Ukrainian dishes.

One evening in autumn, Dr. Frick came to see me and he told me about an upcoming meeting in New York of an Assembly of New York Anesthesiologists. "Would you like to go to the meeting with me?" he asked. I went with him and his wife, and boy did I have a ball! They had their own room on the second or third floor, and mine was not very far away. It was a very beautiful hotel. The food was wonderful, delicious. And then they took me to a Broadway show, and I couldn't even close my mouth it was so wonderful. Then we went for a delicious dinner. We stayed from Monday till Friday, and I was able to go visit my parents in New Jersey.

* * * * *

I want to add something about the medical profession. I hope some of my younger colleagues will read this. Medicine is progressing very fast and very well. But what's wrong with the doctors and physicians? Dr. Frick once said to me. "Mary, never, never, never become a hospital employee.Why? Because once you become an employee you lose your own personality. You have to be dependent on administrators, and administrators know nothing or very little about medicine, even though they think they do.

"Those administrators will tell you when to come to work, when to finish the work, how much money they will pay, and God forbid that you ask for a raise. They may never give it to you and they might even fire you. If you don't smile the way they think you should, they might fire you. And when you want a vacation, the administrator will tell you when to go. In other words, you will never be anything but an administrator's employee." And then Dr. Frick said, "In all of my life, even if I didn't make much, I always was self employed." And don't forget this, you guys; in the future being self-employed may be no more.

And over time, now I can see that he was a fortune teller because now the administrators are in control and all the doctors are dependent on them. They are nothing but employees and are totally dependent on the administrators. You might not believe this but the administrators in my time, when I was starting to work, the administrators were just nothing. They were the ones who helped the doctors, because it was a doctor who was chief of the department. And the doctors told the administrators what to do and when to do it. Now the administrators are very well-educated in all aspects of medicine, and in some hospitals, they are very, very well-paid. Some of them even earn more than a banker. And in my opinion, this is a crying shame and I will say, "Shame on the medical profession." I can't understand why the medical profession and the doctors have let themselves fall that low. I hope that some of you younger doctors will read what I have written and open your eyes and start to move the medical field in the right direction.

* * * * *

Dr. Frick was Chief of the Anesthesiology Department and was a wonderful, wonderful person, to me anyway. When I was finishing my residency, he came to wish me lots of luck. He told both me and George that he was going to help us in any way he could. He said that he would write recommendation papers for me, and true to his word, I got excellent recommendation papers from him. He was very smart and very good to me and I adored him. I used to write to him for a long, long time, and he always answered me until one day he stopped and I found out that he had died. I still pray for Dr. Frick all the time.

During my meetings in New York, I also visited George's sisters for a short visit. They had both moved to better apartments, clean and beautiful and a nice view. Paula had met a priest from the Ukrainian parish and the priest found a position with the Catholic school. Boy, was Paula happy she did not have to clean any longer. That priest, Patrick Pashchak, became a very good friend of both our families.

My father was happy too because he had started his parish with only ten people and he found a place in an old Methodist Church that he could rent for very little money. My father rented that parish with the understanding that if anything broke, he would have to fix it. Then two years later, my father bought the old church. Then he opened a Sunday School and all of my family became involved in that school. In about two years they had over one hundred students.

It was too far for him to go back and forth from that place. His church was located on Plum Street. So he rented an apartment from an old Hungarian couple who lived just across the street from his church. Finally, my father bought himself an old used car. He kept it for two or three years and then he changed to a new Packard. My father was in heaven due to the parish and his wonderful new car. It was nineteen fifty-five and Father was almost sixty. It was a miracle that he succeeded so well.

Then big trouble came. The first year of George's residency, the Korean War broke out and George was "invited" to join "Uncle Sam". We didn't know what to do and then I remembered Dr. Schoiker. I knew him because he was my boss in pathology training. I remembered seeing him in an army uniform with all of his military medals. I sent George to talk to him.

George came home all happy and he felt much better. Dr. Schoiker helped George fill out all his papers, and George was accepted in the Army Reserves and he had to go once a year to Camp Drum in New York. George was so happy about all that.

At that time, interns and residents all had to go for special CPR training at the Western Reserve Hospital in Ohio. In those days, you must cut open the chest and massage the heart. It's not like now. We had only two or three weeks of training and they usually performed the operation on dogs. I felt sorry for the animals and I was glad when that was over. Finally, we got certificates and we were trained.

Dr. Frick took me more than once to meetings in Cleveland and it was much nicer than three weeks at the Western Reserve. I also went three or four times to New York City with him.

Now we found out that if you do not have your state boards, you cannot practice medicine. Then, before we could take our state boards, we found out that we must take two separate exams in English and history. I passed history and English just fine. And also, if you are a foreign graduate, you must take State Board Exams in each state.

Then we returned to Columbus and I took my state boards. We assumed that we would pass everything. We took the state boards that spring and the exams were horrible.

It was now July, nineteen fifty-five, and now it was time for us to pass the United States Immigration Test. I couldn't wait to take that test. I passed it and now I can open my mouth because finally, I belonged to a place. I cried, I laughed, and I can do what I want. Now I am a human being and finally an American citizen!

There is no country in the whole world that can give you as much as this country! There is no country on the face of this earth that will take better care of you than the United States of America. This I truly believe until the day I die. AMEN! AMEN! AMEN!

Before we left Ohio, my husband bought us a new Chevrolet car for five hundred dollars. We packed and returned to New Jersey to my parents' home. We went to church, and then everybody began to ask questions about us and why two doctors weren't working. Now I didn't know what to do. We hadn't passed our state boards and my mother was getting very worried.

We took our exams again, and within six months, we learned that we had both passed. We went to Trenton, and I have always been very outspoken. I told the physician who was President of the Medical Society that I came to get reciprocity. And he told me that they do not accept German medical diplomas after World War Two—we both were declined, and I was so upset.

What could we do now? My mother did not want us to leave. Some friend advised George that he could prolong his New Jersey studies. I found a job in a New Jersey hospital in Irvington. It was a very small hospital with two hundred beds. I still had no license in New Jersey but I worked with a Dr. Ben Jacobs. It was a very good job and everyone was so nice to me. In the meantime, George got more training in the Seaton Hall in Jersey City.

I was finally earning nice money so we moved to an East Orange condominium that was mostly inhabited by professional people. It was like living in heaven to me. It was a clean, modern apartment. One day an ambulance driver invited us to his home and we met his family. His brother-in-law Joe was in the process of buying a car dealership. Joe was very friendly with us and he was very Irish. His mother was still alive and they became good friends of ours.

George had finally finished his extra training and my mother was still so worried that we would leave New Jersey. Maria, my cousin, got a scholarship to the Sorbonne, in Paris, France and she left to study French Literature.

George decided to return to Ohio. I didn't want to go back there. George found out that Rhode Island is very close to New Jersey so we went to Rhode Island and took the Rhode Island State Boards. But after we passed the boards, I couldn't find a job. We didn't know what to do. It didn't work out for us there.

In the meantime, George met a Ukrainian physician and he was so happy to meet him. He told George that he lives in Maine and it wasn't a big city, but he works under excellent conditions at a psychiatric hospital. He was sure that George would love it there. He told George that, "Augusta, Maine is God's country," and George really wanted to go there.

He took his car and left right away for Maine. Joe gave me a fifty-dollar car and now I could drive too. I thought that George would come back and tell me that it was a horrible place and he would not live there. To my surprise, he came back with a lobster for me and he loved Maine! He had only good news for me.

Then he said to me, "Mary, next week I will take my Maine State Boards." I was very unhappy that he still wanted to go to live in Maine. He passed his state boards the first time and then he was told that in Lewiston they desperately needed an obstetrics and gynecology physician as soon as possible. He loved everything about Maine. What could I say; he packed his suitcase and he went. Now the Mother Superior at St. Mary's Hospital is waiting for me to come too. Guess what—I told George that I wasn't going with him. I guess I tried to scare him because I really didn't want a divorce.

George found a rent in downtown Lewiston and he came back to pack the rest of his things around the end of October. In November, I took a few days off to go visit George. I took a bus to New York City and then a train to Portland, Maine. George came to meet me and we had a discussion about what we were going to do. And then we came to Lewiston. George's office was very small and it also was his apartment,

One month later, he had no patients, nobody would come. Joe loaned George some money to move to another office. Then I got to the hospital where we met Dr. L. He was very quiet, shy or bashful as the chief of the department. St. Mary's Hospital at that time was only a forty-bed hospital.

Old Boys Hockey Team – this was meant for George. They built a big, strong hockey team; he was like an alcoholic and he couldn't be changed. Now, I told him that I was leaving and I didn't think I would come to Lewiston. When I returned to New Jersey, my boss called me and told me that he was not allowed to keep any physician who did not have a license in New Jersey. That meant that I would return to Maine, and boy, was George happy, but I was still very upset.

I worked in New Jersey until the beginning of February and then I came to Lewiston. George had a chance to take three small apartments and turn them into a professional medical office. He hired a nurse and then a secretary. When I got there and saw what he had done, I was very surprised. His specialty was in obstetrics/gynecological, not general practitioner. Lewiston was a boom town at that time; they had more jobs than workers.

One of George's first patients came to see him because she had been told that she would never conceive. Within five years, that lady had three children and she sent him many patients from the shoe factory. George was so happy, and after five years, he built a very nice new office at 300 Pine Street in Lewiston.

George called to tell me that he had found a duplex house with a beautiful garden and a garage. I went to see it, but I was very heartbroken and very unhappy. George came to see me in New Jersey and he packed everything in the car, and we had the movers bring the furniture to Maine.

When I got to St. Mary's Hospital, they were very nice to me, and I wanted to find my anesthesia equipment because I wanted to see where and what I would be working with. Now the trouble starts when I finally saw the medical equipment. It was obsolete and so backwards. The sister who ran the operating room thought she knew it all.

The mother superior signed me to a salary of four hundred dollars a month, and I was introduced to Dr. L. Now the most important part— the equipment seemed two hundred years behind. I was in a state of shock. I was used to the best equipment—the best of everything. There were no good endotracheal tubes. Where was the children's equipment? What would we do if a child stops breathing? How do we administer oxygen to the child? All the next day, I was looking for an IV Ringer solution and a Foley catheter. In this unit, all of the medical equipment should not be reused.

Then I had an argument with the mother superior about the equipment and I demanded that we have new, modern equipment. Two weeks passed and there still was no new equipment. I went to see mother superior to tell her that I was leaving. She asked me what was wrong and I told her that we had waited nearly two weeks and we didn't have any new equipment. The very next day, at eight a.m., the medical equipment salesman called me and I gave him my order. I only wanted the best for my department. I got everything I wanted. I told the sister in charge in the operating room that I was going to be the boss and all of the medical supplies after one use would be discarded.

Then I laid down the law to George, too. In one or two or three years I will return to New Jersey. I hate this place! Then maybe two or three weeks later I got a call from the Daughters of Italy Club. Thinking that I was of Italian heritage, they invited me to have dinner with them. I agreed and in a few days they called me asking if I am Italian. You would not believe it but they cancelled their invitation.

After being employed at St. Mary's about two or three months, an older surgeon came and slapped me on the shoulder and told me to get him a coffee. I turned and looked at him and told him that he could get his own coffee!

Dr. L and I were invited to all our surgical meetings and they still had no chief of anesthesia. Some surgeons came over from Central Maine Medical Center to attend the meeting. Dr. K, who was a general surgeon and a chief of the department, asked Dr. L to be chief of anesthesia. After Dr. L declined, I was very proud of myself and I told them that I wanted to the chief. "A woman chief! You mean temporary?" "No, not temporary." "Maybe it would be better if a man takes over," the male doctors all said. But Dr. L told them that I should be chief. Boy, did all the old doctors shut up!

Then trouble came when Dr. L put a patient to sleep and I heard the patient slept for two days before he finally woke up. Three doctors went to see the mother superior to tell her what had happened. They thought that I had put the patient to sleep. They came to see me, too, and I told them, "Don't forget, you have an old person with many, many medical conditions and to help them they have to be under deep anesthesia. Since you have to use so many drugs and the surgery is so long, sometimes you cannot help it." When they found out that it was Dr. L who had put the patient to sleep, they were very apologetic and ashamed.

My George was in seventh heaven. He was very busy in his practice and in hockey. Then one of our physicians went to Augusta to make a complaint against George. They complained that he was an obstetrician & gynecology doctor and he should not take care of the team's injuries. George told them that he only took care of the team's minor injuries. He told them that he was only being a Good Samaritan, and after that everything was okay. Unfortunately, he played only a few more years and then he stopped, but he was their doctor until the end. But he skated for a long time and he skied too. He fell in love with Lost Valley Ski Mountain. I was always in the beginner level in skiing.

Dr. L really wasn't happy at St. Mary's. He was shy and would not speak up. He came to see me several times and he complained about his superiors. But you know, as chief, you have to speak up and you have to fight with everything you have. And you have to be very outspoken, which he was not. He was so shy and so timid. I couldn't believe that a man could be like that because I was not used to seeing a shy and timid man. All the men I had ever known in my life were very outspoken.

Finally, after coming to see me many times to complain about his superiors, he said that they were horrible to him. I told him that they weren't horrible, they were just ignorant. They didn't know anything about anesthesia. They think that you put a little medicine in the tube and the patient wakes up when they want to. But they don't know the many problems you can have with the medication and how much you have to give them.

When I was working, I could see that Dr. L was very unhappy in his position and with the hospital in general. And I became very scared that if he leaves, there will be only me. Along with Dr. L, there was only Theresa, a Certified Nurse Anesthetist, and myself—just three of us in the Anesthesiology Department.

At that time Lewiston was so backwards in regard to medical technology. They did not know what an anesthetist or an anesthesiology doctor really was. Their mentality was that usually the surgeon put his patients to sleep himself. And there was the question of salary. I think that I was getting about four hundred dollars a month, and Dr. L was getting much more—but of course, he was "chief of anesthesiology" and a "man", and at that time, no matter what your training was, a woman didn't get as much money as a man.

Another problem was that the other doctors had seen me put their patients to sleep and they began calling me instead of him. And I didn't blame him for being upset; after all, he was an anesthesiologist and had much more training than me.

I had only been at Saint Mary's Hospital about two months when one morning when I went to work, Sister F called me to her office and believe me, she was something else. She was a smart nurse but she was also a trouble maker. She told me to come to her office and as I walked there, I worried about what I might have done.

When I walked into her office, she told me to sit down because if I remained standing, I might faint. I thought that somebody had died or was very sick from my anesthesia. To this very day, I have never forgotten what she said. She said, "Guess what? Dr. L came to see the Mother Superior this morning and told her he was leaving." I wondered to myself why he hadn't come to say goodbye to me too, we had never had any problems. She said that she didn't know why he had left. She told me that he had gone over to work at the Central Maine Medical Center where he stayed for about a year and then he and his family left to go back to New Hampshire.

I didn't know if I should faint, commit suicide, or just die because now I am alone at St. Mary's with only that young nurse and I didn't know what to do next. I wanted to leave too, but what could I do, George was so happy in Lewiston it was like someone had given him a million dollars. So I told the sister that we would have to do as little as possible. We had two rooms to run, and on the major cases I would do them, and on the minor ones, Theresa would take care of them. It was too much for only two people. But the sister told me that we couldn't do that because they had three operating rooms and the emergency room, too.

We were lucky because when I came to Saint Mary's they had some very smart, good surgeons and I liked them all and I never had any problems with them. There was Dr. Morin, Dr. Clouthier, Dr. Martel and Dr. Fishman who was a thoracic surgeon and he would come to help the other surgeons whenever we needed extra help. There was also Dr. James, Dr. Swett, Dr. Lidstone, and last but certainly not least, Dr. George Dycio. I would also like to mention Danny Isabell, who was my pupil, and I chose him to go to anesthesia school. He was very dedicated to me, and when I had my ninetieth birthday last year on July tenth, he came with his wife to give me their blessings. I was very upset when he died in the winter of two thousand and twelve at the age of eighty.

Now what could we do about the anesthesia doctor? I could not do everything by myself. I couldn't commit suicide. So I called my best advisor, George Dycio. I had seldom seen him get upset and he counseled me very well. He told me, "Mary, Mary, take it easy. They should be glad they have you."

Then somebody told me to call Maine Medical Center in Portland, Maine, and so I did. I talked to a Dr. L and he told me that he felt sorry for me. Then he thought of a Dr. Margaret. She had just finished her training and she had seven kids. He gave me her telephone number and so I called her.

She was very nice to me and she thought she might be able to come for two or three days a week. She was very smart but very slow. Finally, somehow, working with Sister F, we changed the operating room schedule and it worked with Dr. Margaret's schedule.

We had one surgeon and he didn't understand even a five-minute delay. He was a stickler about beginning on time. But Margaret lived in Portland and she was always held up in traffic. She was a horrible driver and she had agreed that she would try to be at our unit at seven a.m., but she was always late. I thought that the operating room surgeon was going to have a nervous breakdown because he paced around the operating room for three hours until Margaret finally arrived. On another day, she didn't arrive until ten thirty and when she walked into our unit, she was carrying a big box. She had brought us a live chicken. A truck had overturned and his entire load of chickens had fallen out of the truck, so she rescued a chicken. Then, she had to go to a store to buy some food for that chicken and she didn't return until eleven o'clock.

One day she volunteered to drive me to a meeting and I was scared to death about her driving. She was always looking around and she drove too close to the ditch. I never wanted to drive anywhere with her again.

I was carrying the whole Anesthesiology Unit because Margaret could not take calls because she had small children. Finally, I found Irene, who was a very good nurse. She worked for an Ear, Nose & Throat doctor, but she wanted to change to anesthesia. Finally, I had someone that I could rely on, and things began to turn around. By now, Margaret was very well-trained and she finally changed from working only two days a week to five days—boy, was I happy!

After a few years, we finally have three operating rooms working. Then, Dr. A, who was an urologist, came to us from the Central Maine Medical Center. He was always good natured and he liked to joke a lot. He told me that he had heard that I was the Chief Anesthesiologist at St. Mary's, and my George told him that it was true. Then Dr. A told me that his wife, Dorothy, was also an anesthesiologist and she had received excellent training at a hospital in Detroit, Michigan.

I called her and Dorothy said that her husband would not allow her to work too many hours because they had seven children. I called her nearly every day for two weeks and finally she capitulated. She was so excellent in her training and very up to date. I wanted so badly for her to come to St. Mary's because I wanted to get rid of those guys that were coming over from the local Locum Tenants, which was an agency that, upon request, sent medical staff to hospitals when their staff was low.

Now, I have Dorothy two or three days a week and Margaret, too. And I am applying everywhere for another anesthesiologist. I finally got lucky and found Dr. A. He was very smart and capable but he was a little on the lazy side. He would sneak off and go home to have a lunch, and I had never even had time for a cup of coffee during the years I had been there. And he was gone for an hour at lunch every day. We called him a "Greek God" because he was spoiled.

I would like to mention something about our nursing staff. When we came to St. Mary's Hospital in nineteen fifty-seven, Nurse Diane had just graduated from nursing school. In those days, you didn't have to go to college because all the medical training was available through the hospitals. The nursing students would study there three years and become a registered nurse with a degree in nursing. To me, they were super, good nurses. They were all overworked and underpaid.

I remember one incident when Sister F was in charge. This is not to blame her but she was in charge. She came to see me. It was six o'clock in the evening and we were finally going home. But she insisted that I stay because one of the doctors had a patient with an emergency. I told her that I would stay because, as head of that department, I really had to stay. Then, one of the nurses told her that she couldn't stay because she wasn't on call and that one of her children was sick. But the sister told the nurse that she had a doctor arriving soon with the patient and she really needed that nurse to stay.

But the nurse said "Sister, I have very small children and my husband goes to work at seven. I have to go babysit!"

Sister F looked at her and said "No! Your job here is first and your kids are last!" That just goes to show that the nuns had no idea about children or family. But that nurse was adamant and she replied, "Sister I must go home! I cannot leave my very small children all alone! I have nobody to babysit for me."

Sister F looked at her and then she said, "Well, if you go, don't ever come back!"

We had excellent nurses in the operating room, and Diane was an excellent nurse. She was divorced with four children and her husband had died after their divorce, so she was chiefly responsible for her children's care. Nurse Diane stayed at St. Mary's Hospital for many, many years just like me. She was an excellent scrub and charge nurse.

At the end, when I was leaving, the new administrator let Diane go because they complained that the hospital didn't have enough money. I really don't know what happened to her because it was really none of my business, but she was so good at her job. I couldn't understand why she had left St. Mary's, but her leaving was really a good thing for her because she went to Portland to the Maine Medical Center and found a job in their modern Cardiac Surgical Department. She must have been brilliant because they also kept her for many, years until she retired.

When I first came to St. Mary's Hospital the whole Anesthesiology Department was in very bad shape. They had forty-five beds, two operating rooms on the second floor, and a little upstairs room that was used for tonsillectomies. We really should not have used that room and we were very lucky that there were no explosions because we had to use ether for the children's anesthesia. But at that time, we didn't have a recovery room. Nobody, from the youngest anesthesiologist to the regular physicians, can even imagine how horrible it was to finish a case sometimes two or three a clock in the morning, and then you had to push the patient yourself from the operating room to the floor. And don't forget in those days, there might be only one large room with twenty or thirty patients in it, and your post-operative patient was still deep under the anesthesia. We didn't have much equipment to help our patients either. There might be some oxygen and blood pressure cuffs, but that was all.

One day I finished a case and brought the patient to his room. I was all alone. There was only one nurse in charge of the whole room. How could she help me take care of my patient? She had to delegate someone like a nurse's aide to help me. I usually went to check on my patient every half hour or so to see how they were doing. Looking back, it seems unimaginable that we actually had to work under such horrible, primitive conditions.

When Dr. L left St. Mary's, I was working like a slave and I talked everything over with George. George was good in everything he did. Before he had his medical degree, he also had a degree in business. He knew that I did not want to stay on the hospital payroll and wanted to be able to bill my own patients. When you work for a hospital you had to depend on someone else for everything. But after about five months I had no money coming in. Nobody wanted to pay. Then I found a collection agency and we finally began to have some money, and finding that agency was the best thing I could have done. I was still waiting and dreaming about returning to New Jersey and going to New York City to the Broadway shows and the restaurants and the shopping. I dearly loved to go shopping and I still do.

Maybe two years passed and we were finally allowed to take our state boards in New Jersey. I told George that we should take our boards and then move back there. But George was not interested in doing that. His medical practice was just beginning to grow, and he had a hockey team here that he loved. He loved Lewiston and he wanted to buy a house here. I told him that I didn't want to live in Lewiston and that I was going back to New Jersey. He told me that it's a free country and I can do what I want, but I really didn't know what I was going to do. All the people who meant so much to me, my parents, my uncle, and George's sisters, were all in New Jersey and New York. I didn't want to stay in Maine but what could I do? I loved my George and I really didn't want to leave him.

I shouldn't have told my mother and father what was going on because they wanted us to move back to New Brunswick, New Jersey. Then my father told me about a house near them that would make us a lovely home. George could not be swayed and he could not be moved. He wasn't going to leave his beloved Maine.

George had a good friend in Augusta, Maine, and he and his wife always invited us to their home for a huge supper. His wife was an excellent cook and I loved going there. I had never learned to cook and I hated it. His friend's wife didn't work outside their home; she had stayed home to raise their child.

Now my father began to hear horrible stories about Stalin and Ukrainian underground. Nobody really knew what had or what was happening to their relatives. George's cousin still had contact with some of our family in Poland and now you could send mail to Poland. And that family would send letters to my father, and they have to be so careful because if Stalin found out that they had relatives living in the United States, Stalin would persecute, eradicate or destroy the whole family.

My father's sister's husband had died, and we think he was killed by the Russians. They had a beautiful farm and a home, and after her husband was killed, my aunt continued to live in their home. But then the Russians came and took all the land they had and their home too. Back then, the Russians would only allow you to have one or two rooms and they would not allow you to live alone unless you were a communist party member.

Doris and her husband Lev had a boy of ten and a little girl about one year old. Her husband was very smart and he had a law degree. Lev was working for a Ukrainian newspaper in Munich but he wanted to leave Germany and come to the United States. Doris had been to the United States before and she didn't like it. They couldn't speak English and I think she knew that if she came to United States they would have to get jobs as manual workers. Doris had never had to work hard and they had always been involved in politics and they were living quite comfortably in Munich.

In the spring of nineteen fifty-seven, my father called me and told me that a terrible tragedy had happened. He said that Doris' husband had been going to his job at the newspaper and that he had a severe heart attack and died on the steps of the office. To all of us, it seemed very suspicious that he had died so suddenly. They performed an autopsy and they found that Lev has suffered a massive heart attack. My father said that he couldn't understand how that could have happened because Lev had already survived two and a half or three years in a German concentration camp.

Then, just like Lev, another Ukrainian freedom fighter, Bandera, was also dead. They were both dead in a very short time, and we always believed that they were killed by the Russians. Now what was Doris going to do? My father had no money to help her. There was nobody who could help. George and I were still making very little money and working very hard. We didn't know what to do to help her. Then Doris and her two children had to move out of their very nice apartment into a smaller place. We felt so bad for them. But in a very short time, through her connections, she found a little secretarial job with the Red Cross and this helped a little. She was a very smart woman and she was a lawyer. She spoke Russian, Ukrainian, German and a little English too.

My poor father had a good heart for everybody and he talked to me about Doris' problem. And my George had a heart of gold too, and even though we had very little money to spare, George and I sent her some money every month to help her. Later on, she told us how that little bit of money had helped her so much.

I am still very unhappy living in Maine, but George doesn't want to return to New Jersey. George was always very stubborn, but I always found a way to get along with him, and he with me. But George felt at home here in Lewiston and I didn't.

George's office looked very nice and he was becoming very busy. I was also working all the time and I was tired, tired, tired. Then in about a year I had to go to Boston to take my Anesthesia Board Exams. I told George that St. Mary's would not allow me to leave because they were always so busy. At that time they were called the board's "fellowship" because they were boards written, oral, and practical boards. I knew that if I told the hospital I was going to take time off to study for my boards, the surgeons would try to stop me. So I decided that I would stay home one week and study and then I would go to Boston. I told George to tell Sister F in the operating room that I was very sick and to leave me alone. I stayed home one whole week and studied, and then I went to Boston. I was very confident that I would pass and I was so happy. About a month later, I received my papers stating that I had passed!

It was now nineteen fifty-nine and we were living in a very nice apartment, but George was getting completely crazy. He wanted to build a house. Again I told him I didn't want to build a house in Maine because I still wanted to return to New Jersey. No matter what I said to him, he was adamant. He wanted a home, he wanted a family, and he wanted a dog. No matter what I said to him he wouldn't change his mind, and I was broken hearted but I finally agreed to accept his decision about building us a home. I thought maybe later on, as years passed and he couldn't play hockey any longer, maybe then he would return with me to New Jersey. But it never happened.

We set about finding a place to build our home. We found a very nice section of town in Lewiston called Maple Ridge and we began to build our house that George wanted so badly, on Bayberry Lane. It was going to have five bedrooms and five bathrooms because being European, your parents live with you when they get old and maybe we will have children.

On April twenty-sixth, nineteen sixty, our oldest son was born and we named him George Myron. He weighed about six pounds and he was very sick with colic, a runny nose and ear aches. We needed someone to care for him and we hired a nanny to come and live with us. She was very good to our baby. When Georgie was born, we were still living in our old duplex, and when he was about six months old, we moved to our beautiful home on Bayberry Lane. Our home had been built on two lots in a residential area, and our property was very beautiful. Now I started to change my mind about staying in Maine and I was becoming very happy with our home.

My parents came to visit us and my father told me "Marusia, be happy and we will be happy too." My father was in seventh heaven because his little parish in New Jersey was growing and he now had many parishioners. And, his church now had about five hundred parishioners. Yes, my parents and especially my father were very happy with their life in New Jersey.

Next, we heard on the radio that Stalin is dead. Hooray! Hooray! The evil devil is dead! My father thought that maybe in one year our Ukraine will be free. After a couple of non-descript leaders, Khrushchev was in power. He was half Ukrainian and he told all the war survivors, "Anyone who wants to return to Ukraine can now go home." Khrushchev was not as terrible as Stalin, and there was no longer a fear of being sent to prison in Siberia. It is now nearing the end of nineteen sixty and we can send letters and small packages to Ukraine. So my father began writing to our relatives, and things began to get easier for our relatives back home.

My aunt and her two girls found a sponsor and they returned to Ukraine from Kazakhstan but they could not find a real job. My aunt and her oldest daughter were not allowed to work as secretaries. The only job they could find was cleaning the streets. So we started to help them, too. The people that Khrushchev freed from imprisonment could return to Ukraine, but only at their own expense.

My aunt's older son, who was a physician, finally made it to the United States and he came to Bayonne, New Jersey and opened his medical practice there. He was so good to his mother and he sent packages for them to Ukraine, and finally she found a job in a meat factory and she started to have a better life. Then in nineteen eighty, my aunt and her nephew came to visit us and she still looked very nice but her legs were very red and swollen from her previous job in Kazakhstan.

Now it was summer and I was scheduled for my oral exams but my they would only be held in Florida because they was a big meeting for the National Anesthesiologist Association scheduled to convene there. Finally after two years of hard work, I flew from Portland, Maine to Miami, Florida, and in just two days, I was finished. I had my fellowship.

It is now the summer of nineteen sixty-three and Georgie began to thrive. So I decided to take a two-week vacation, but George could not take a vacation with me. He had to go to Camp Drum in New York for his four weeks on his medical duty. I didn't complain because he was in the reserves, and it was better than our lives would have been if we had stayed in Ukraine. Then my George took his written board exam in Augusta and he passed.

Now, my poor mother was always complaining because the glue that she used in the factory where she had worked for so long had caused her to lose all of her fingernails. Her poor hands hurt her all the time. I felt so sorry for her that I promised her that I would send her a little money as soon as I could. And finally, at the age of sixty-two, she was able to stop working. She was so ashamed that she did not have any finger nails; she would always wear gloves when she went out to shop or go anyplace.

In nineteen sixty, at St. Mary's, they opened a big new hospital wing with three-hundred beds. St. Mary's little hospital overnight became something to really be proud of. We now had five large operating rooms with a sixth room for lesser emergencies, and they even built a special room for the anesthetists to stay in, not to mention a beautiful recovery room for all of our patients. This new hospital was a blessing from another place.

At St. Mary's, Margaret quit her job to stay home and take care of her children, and we began looking for another anesthesiologist to take her place. George asked me why I didn't open a school for nurse anesthetists. He thought it would be very easy. I did have a secretary and she helped me fill out all the papers I needed to open the school. And you don't know how many forms we had to fill out in order to get approved for a school. And stupid me, I opened my school. Then, I received a letter that the inspectors were coming to check to see if everything was good. And to see if we were qualified to even run a school.

The woman who was in charge of our evaluation had been in the military or something like that and she was horrible to deal with. Her associate, a man, was just as nasty as she was. They checked and rechecked all of our machines and they asked so many questions and made so much trouble for us. They were on our backs from morning until night. They told me we needed more nurses to help run the school. They didn't want to allow just anyone to open a "mediocre" school. And we had to take them to lunch and she always asked for lobster. And I secretly hoped that she would choke on her lobster!

I asked her why she was giving us so much trouble about opening our school and she told me that they couldn't allow just "anyone" to open a school because all the schools they approved had to be "excellent" in all respects.

Finally, after what seemed like a lifetime to me, a couple of months later, we received our permit to open the school. Boy, everything was so involved with reports, reports, and reports. Every week that we were in operation I had to write a report. I was so sorry that George had ever suggested that I open a school. I couldn't understand why I had to write so many papers if I wanted to teach anesthesia. But my secretary was very excellent and she helped me so much with all the reports and papers that I had to complete. I was so lucky to have found her because now I was doubly busy working with my school "and" St. Mary's.

Now I have my first son, my little Georgie, and I had my hands full. My lovely little boy had colic, colic, colic and ear aches. I was so tired, I was dizzy. Then one day, I was at my house and George came home all smiles. He had good news for a change. My George had a very nice lady who was his patient and she was interested in helping us with our family. So we hired her to be our housekeeper and nanny. She was very good to my Georgie, and if I asked her to cook some little food for us she did a good job in that too. After about two years, she started to fall ill and when she left us, we hired Mrs. G.

In nineteen sixty-two, our second son Mark was born, and again, just like his big brother Georgie, he was sickly right from the start. Mrs. G was also George's patient and we were lucky to find her. She had grown children and she had been working in a local shoe factory, like half of the population in the Lewiston area, and she was also an excellent cook. She was elderly and she worked so hard for us and she was a wonderful lady. I was very happy to have her.

When Georgie was about five and Mark about three, Mrs. G came to tell me that she was growing old and now her work with us was too much for her. She had to leave us to go live with her daughter who needed her.

Then we found Ms. M, who was an old maid and very French. She always called me, "Madam Dycio." She weighed about three hundred and fifty pounds and she was not a very good cook, but our sons adored her and she really knew how to play with our children. She'd let them crawl onto her heavy lap and she'd tell them stories from morning till night. And she loved to play all kinds of games with them. She took them for walks and even to the circus when it came to town.

Then my George bought a poodle dog for the kids and they called him "Bibi." They really loved that dog, but that dog hated to go for a ride in any car. He was a very nervous dog and you could not bring him in a car or go for a ride. He would scratch that car to pieces trying to get out. He damaged our two cars very severely in the fourteen years that he lived with us. Then he started to fall ill and he developed cancer and we lost him.

As my boys grew older, they wanted all kinds of creatures like rabbits, snakes, and turtles so my boys had all kinds of pets and they had a wonderful life. As soon as the boys were old enough, George took them to a special school to learn to ice skate so that they could learn to play hockey like he did. George loved sports so much and he wanted them to love sports too. My boys were always busy with their sports and their religion. We sent them to St. Joseph's Kindergarten in

Auburn, which was a very French Catholic private school, for their first six years. Because of George's and my heavy work schedules, we had to hire a taxi to pick them up and take them to school in the morning and bring them home at night.

Ms. M usually ate four breakfasts and then I knew why she was so overweight. And she also smoked like a chimney and I didn't like her smoking, so she used to go outside to smoke. She stayed with us three years and then she moved to Rhode Island to live with her niece. We were very sad when she told us she was leaving because she had worked so well for us, and back then, it wasn't easy to find someone like her.

Then we hired Mrs. O to come and work for us, and you won't believe it because she stayed with us for eighteen years. She was the mother of ten children, and her husband had died when her youngest son was only two years old. She then went to work in a local shoe factory and she stayed there until she was sixty-five. When she retired from that job, my hairdresser recommended her to me. So I called her up and she agreed to come work for us, but she told me in the very beginning that she would only work for us for a couple of weeks or until I could find someone else. She was a wonderful cook and a wonderful lady and I was so lucky to have found her, and my boys loved her too. Both little Georgie and Mark called her, "Ma." Not only was she an excellent cook, she was an excellent seamstress, a cleaning lady and a gardener. You name it, she could do it.

If George and I were busy at the hospital, we never had to worry one second about our boys. She would help them with their homework, and I had no worries at all about my children's care. As I said before, she stayed with us for eighteen years and then she began having dizzy spells and her health started to fail. She was eighty-two or eighty-three years old when she finally left us. I will never forget her and all the things she did for our family.

I tried so hard to be a good mother to my two sons and I even tried to teach them Ukrainian. I dearly wanted them to be able to speak and understand my language and the history of my country. But my time at home with them was so little that I felt pulled apart by the hospital and my responsibilities at home. All of my life was taken up by work, work and more work. I didn't go to play golf, or join coffee klatches, and I didn't play tennis. I had zero time for a social life. Between my hospital responsibilities, my studies, and my family, there was more work than I could do.

Sometimes, when my children were very small, I used to have a terrible guilt complex and thought I should stop working and be a "real" mother. But then I fought with myself about work or don't work. And I knew that if I stopped working for three years or so, my profession status wouldn't be any good any more. I would have to go back to Boston or New York for refresher courses because Lewiston was too small to have them. And that would have been out of the question for me. So I decided to take a nice deep breath and do the best I could under those circumstances.

George was still performing operations and he always amazed me with his surgical ability. He could take the most complicated operation and make it seem easy. His hands and fingers were made for a surgeon. I envied him and his surgical ability.

Finally, with a new home and two beautiful sons, I was growing very, very happy with my life. When our boys were small, if there was a meeting, George and I could not attend it together because someone needed to be at home with the boys. And we were always afraid that if we went away together, there might be an accident, and God forbid, our children would lose both parents. That's why, when I had to attend a medical conference, I always chose the best place that I could so that I could learn as much as possible. I went to New Orleans, New York, Chicago and California. I used to go, but that was not pleasant for me, and it was not fun to be alone. Yes, I met a lot of people on my trips, but I was always on my own.

As our boys grew and became teenagers and were better able to care for themselves, then George and I started to travel together. That time and those trips we took together were the best times of our lives. We always tried to attend excellent, up-to-date meetings and conferences, but not just in Boston or New York. We were now able to attend medical conventions in Hungary, Germany, France, Italy, Finland, Mexico, and many in the southern islands and Aruba. We always had such a wonderful time, met so many lovely people, and had the best of food that we couldn't wait for the next meeting.

When George and Mark were both at Hebron Academy, they had many, many friends. Some would come and visit us because they came from very far away. And we always had an open house and heart for them. One of those friends, was a boy named Troy. Somehow, he is still friendly with Mark. When Mark and his family come to visit me, Troy and his family always come to see them too. Troy is in the restaurant business and maybe twice a year he invites me to join them for a supper.

But, I do want to say this. When we went to France, the other doctors treated us very well. But there was one time, when we went to a meeting with about twenty or fifty other doctors from the United States, which will stay in my memory forever. We had been invited to dinner at a local French restaurant and our entire group of doctors was speaking English. The waitresses were all so mean to us and we couldn't understand why. Hadn't our soldiers died so that France could be independent, and those waitresses didn't even smile or try to be friendly. They were throwing the plates and silverware onto our tables. So George told me to follow him out and we went and sat in the dining area entrance and we began speaking very loudly in our Ukrainian language. When the wait staff heard this, suddenly they were happy and smiling at us. They said, "Oh, you speak Ruskie!" And George told them, "No! We are not Russian! We are Ukrainian!"

Both George and I couldn't get over how rude the French were. They should have been nice and friendly. If it hadn't been for the Americans, they would probably still be under Germany's regime until today. Didn't they realize that? Of all the countries that we visited, France was the only place where the citizens were not nice to us Americans. Maybe we went to the wrong restaurant, I don't know. But Finland, Sweden, Italy and Hungary were so wonderful to us. We never traveled just the two of us, we always went with a whole group of American physicians.

As I said before, my boys were nearly grown, and one day my mother called me. It was early on a Monday morning in July of nineteen sixty-seven. I will never forget that date, or her phone call. She called to tell me that my wonderful father had suddenly passed away. That was a horror for her and for us because I was always very close to my father. During his later years, he had helped me so much; he was my councilor and my advisor. I had always listened to him, all of my life. I dearly loved both of my parents, but both my grandmother and my father were very "special" to me.

That was a horrible, horrible tragedy because my father was only seventy-nine and was in excellent health. He had had two or three mild heart attacks in the past but never had to have any heart procedures. He died suddenly, because on that fateful morning, he had awakened and he had asked my mother for some water. She went to get him the water and when she came back, he was gone.

His funeral was very beautiful and there were hundreds of people, including other priests and even a bishop, who came to pay their last respects. My father was always a very loveable man and he had organized that little parish into one of the best attended Ukrainian parishes in New Jersey. He had organized the Catholic Sunday School and it now had over one hundred students and both my mother and my uncle ran the school. When he had first arrived in New Jersey, he rented a little chapel and then he was able to buy it. Then he worked until he was able to buy a large church that was almost a cathedral. And behind the church there was a huge building that had rooms and offices for other priests to stay in and work. His church was a gorgeous place. It was located in the middle of New Brunswick and this parish blossomed under my father's guidance. My father was always so very proud of his accomplishments and now he was dead. Oh, my heart was broken.

My mother never was a lady who could take care of herself. My father always had to tell her what to do. She tried to drive a car but she never could learn. They had a beautiful six room house and now my mother was very lonely. My aunt and my cousin wanted to move in to be with her, but my mother was determined that she was going to come and live with us in Maine. I was only able to take one week off and I stayed in New Jersey to help my mother pack and put her home for sale. In that week, I had to pack everything that she wanted to keep and remove it from the house.

I stayed with her in New Jersey until the following Saturday and I told my mother that she should go to live with my aunt. I tried to tell her that she really wasn't going to like living in Maine because she didn't know anybody. In New Jersey, she had her church where the parishioners all knew her and they all loved and respected her. But my mother said that she wasn't going to stay there. She was always afraid and very frightened to be alone and she was determined that she was going to come to Maine and live with us.

I placed the house for sale and in just one month, we were able to sell it for only forty-five thousand. To me, that was just like giving it away. Anyway, the new owners moved in and then their sale didn't go through. They left our house damaged and dirty, and once we'd made the necessary repairs and repainted it, we lowered the price to thirty-five thousand and it finally sold for good, one month later.

Once mother was living with us in Maine, she became very, very unhappy. Both George and I were still working fulltime and our boys were in school every day. We still had our housekeeper, Mrs. O, and she had to do everything in our home, all the cooking, the washing, the ironing, the cleaning and all of the other jobs that George and I weren't there to do. And Mrs. Ouellette really couldn't understand my mother's speech.

My poor mother was always complaining and complaining all day long. She kept asking both George and me, "Why do you stay at your work so long?" And, "Why don't you come home earlier so we can go out for some ice cream or something, or maybe we can go to the movies." The only real happiness she had was that once in a while, I would take her back home to New Jersey and she would stay there two or three days, visit all of her old friends, and then she would come crying back to Maine.

There was one other thing that she liked. There was a Ukrainian summer resort Souzivka, near Kingston, New York and we would take her with us when we went to Fort Drum, New York for George's reserve obligations. We also took our boys there so that they could attend their Boy Scout camp. My mother and my aunt loved to visit that place and they went there for two summers. And one of George's sisters, who was nearly my mother's age, went and stayed there with my mother for nearly a month, and they enjoyed it very much. Of course, it cost me a lot of money because they stayed so long, but I was happy that my mother was happy even if it didn't last too long. My mother especially loved it there because of all the wonderful food and she got to meet so many Ukrainian people. And all the singing brought back many happy memories to her. But coming back to stay in Lewiston was terrible for her because she had no real friends there.

Then, Mrs. O retired at the age of eighty-three and my mother told us that she wasn't going to stay alone. Although she was still quite capable of caring for herself, she wasn't going to. So we had to hire somebody else and we found Mrs. R. She would come and stay with my mother from eight in the morning until one of us returned that day. Mrs. R had her own car and she was a beautiful companion for my mother. She would take mother out for lunch and then they'd go shopping together. She had been a nurse's aide and she had worked in a nursing home and she really knew how to handle my mother. Mother, now at the age of eighty-five, was beginning to get senile little by little. Though mother was an excellent cook, after father died and she had moved to my house, she didn't want to cook any more. She really didn't want to do anything at all. She cried all the time because she now had lost her husband and her son had died at a very young age.

My cousin Doris, whose husband had been killed by the Russians, finally retired from her job. he had worked for many years for the Red Cross in Germany and she would come to visit us from time to time. She'd stay maybe a month or six weeks, and my mother loved her so much. Mrs. R would take the two of them and drive them everywhere they wanted to go. And that was a big relief for me because now that mother had Doris to care about, she wasn't complaining quite so much. From the very day that mother had learned that my young brother had been killed, she was never the same. Although my father always knew how to talk to her to lift her out of her depression, somehow, I was never able to do that for her.

Then, mother began to have many little strokes and she was failing very rapidly. She could no longer speak coherently. In nineteen eighty-nine, she had such a severe stroke that it left her paralyzed and she could no longer speak. She was in the hospital for about two weeks and Dr. L told us that we would no longer be able to care for her. She needed to go to a nursing home because she needed twenty-four hour nursing care and she couldn't care for herself. So we placed her in the D'Youville Pavilion that was run by St. Mary's Hospital, and my conscience is clear because George and I went to see her every chance we had. And I really must say that her care was very excellent in every respect. They were very good to my mother.

Both George and I knew many of the nuns who worked there, and they would take her to the solarium every afternoon and they had a television for her to watch but she could no longer see. My mother was just as good a person as my father had been and he didn't suffer before he died. My mother had to live through not only the death of her only son and her husband, but now she had to suffer with all her horrible, horrible medical problems as well. I used to ask myself why the Good Lord was doing this to her. My lovely mother died in March of nineteen ninety-two. May she forever rest in peace and may God bless her soul.

Well, the days slid by, my father and my mother died and George's brother-in-law also died very suddenly of cancer of the pancreas. Our family was shifting and changing. Meaning, the new generation was coming up.

Then to our surprise, about two months after my mother's death, our Doris also died very suddenly from a severe stroke. When Ukraine finally became independent, her children brought both Doris and Lev back to be buried in their homeland. Now Doris and her husband rest in peace in Ukraine.

I don't know if I have mentioned this before but we decided to buy an old camp in Auburn that was situated on the lovely Taylor Pond. And for my George and the boys, this place was heaven. Our boys were now seven and five and they loved it there. The old camp wasn't so bad and it was located right on the lake. We bought that old place for only eight thousand dollars and it seemed like paradise to us. We decided that probably we had better remodel and install electric heat in the old camp because the nights were still quite cold. So the very first thing we did was to install a telephone and then we installed electricity. We didn't have a well or running water there so we had to bring fresh water with us every time we stayed.

Soon the cool weather had changed and it was getting much warmer and my boys were crying, pleading and begging to go into the water. They were in seventh heaven, swimming, swimming, swimming, water, water, water. That was all they lived for. Then George decided that he wanted a boat and we bought a big, beautiful yellow boat with room enough to hold six people and we were all so happy. Then we built a dock, and even though George had so little time to spare, he used to take the boys out in the boat every chance he got. He would drive them all around the lovely pond, and whenever I had a little spare time, I'd go down and sit on the dock in the bright sunshine.

I was very lucky because I could always trust Mrs. O to take good care of them. She had all kinds of rules and regulations. They were not allowed to go near or into the water when they were alone or if it was raining. She was very strict and if they misbehaved, she would send them to their rooms and not allow them to go out until we came home.

As they grew older, like all the other kids who lived around the pond, George bought them some motor powered boats and a sail boat. And I had never seen in all my life so many kids my boy's age. They all loved to come to our house and play with our boys because Mrs. O was so kind. She always gave all the kids sandwiches and something to drink. The kids loved that and they loved her too. One of our neighbors had two boys, Robbie and Tommy, and they were the same ages as Georgie and Mark. They also attended Hebron Academy and we were very friendly with their parents.

When George's family found out that we now had a summer camp, boy were they happy. Sometimes we had as many as twenty people at our home during the summer time. For them, it was like living in a "free" motel. Usually we would go to the camp at the beginning of May and stay there through the end of October. Sometimes the kids would sleep outside in their tent or on the porch.

Because George's sister Paula was now a teacher, she had the summers off and she was a wonderful help to take care of our children and to cook. This meant that Mrs. O could leave to visit her family or take a vacation. With Paula at my home, this allowed me to take a two-week vacation at Souzivka near Kingston, New York, or the Catskills. I was so very thankful to her for giving me this opportunity to rest.

When my father was still alive, my parents would come and stay with us at the pond a couple of weeks every summer. This made me very happy because they would speak Ukrainian to my boys and try to teach them about their Ukrainian heritage and history. And my father taught the boys about our religion too. And I was so thankful that my parents were visiting, and I had the lovely Mrs. O to help take care of all of them.

When we came to Maine, we knew that there were no Ukrainians or a Ukrainian Church. But one day, we had a visitor, a young priest from Lisbon Falls, a small town next to Lewiston, and he was a parish priest in a Slovak Church in Lisbon. His name was Rev. Fabian. We were so surprised because we did not know that within fifteen miles from Lewiston there was a large Slovak community with their own church, St. Cyril's & Methodius and Priest. And because we always had a very soft heart for those people, we joined the parish. Unfortunately, a few years after that, the father was transferred to another Slovak community in Montreal and two years later, he died from a heart attack. But we always belonged to that church until around two thousand when all three churches combined, and I still belong to that church to this day.

Sometimes, when I was "on call" or something serious was about to happen with patients, I would stay at my house on Bayberry Lane in Lewiston so that I would be available for any emergency surgery. In summer it usually took us about forty-five minutes to drive from our camp to the hospital. I had fought for years and years to have a small extra room in the hospital for the staff to rest in. But the hospital didn't want to give up a non-occupied room because they were so short on space for our patients. I didn't need too much space; I usually slept in my chair in the anesthesia room until I was needed.

In the meantime, George and I could see that the nuns were slowly disappearing. Sometimes they were a "pain in the neck" because they were so strict, but the hospital was thriving. Generally, they respected the physicians and they were kind to me and the other doctors. In later years, it seemed that the hospital administrators did not show respect for their physicians like the old nuns had.

I remember many times when I was making my rounds, I would go into a room to see a patient, and because we had so many patients, the nurses used to get up and find the chart for me. The nurses usually found the correct chart for the correct patient. And to me, this was a sign of real respect.

It was always so that a nun was "in charge" on the floors. Now many of the nuns were getting older and many had returned to their Nunnery in Sherbrook, Canada. The nuns had a nursing home, St. Mary's D'Youville Pavilion, adjacent to the hospital and they were getting more involved in the nursing home. Sister Rachael was very smart and she used to work in the accounting office at the hospital. And then the nuns made her administrator at St. Mary's Hospital. She was very good and she tried in many ways to update the hospital. She opened a psychiatric clinic and then we found a couple of psychiatrists and they began using shock treatments on their patients. And we performed anesthesia for the physicians. Later on, Sister Rachael, because she was so independent, left her religious order in Canada and she returned to Lewiston and became a "lay" person in business.

Somehow, financially and business wise, the hospital was thriving. But after Sister Rachael left, the hospital administrators were always changing. Then some "brothers" came from Chicago and they too, didn't last very long. After the brothers left, the nuns asked the Bishop of Portland to take over and he agreed. But after a few years, it was too much for him. St. Mary's changed their name and it was now to be called the St. Mary's Hospital under Covenant Health Systems. Every time we turned around, we had a new hospital administrator. We were very busy and I really couldn't complain. Now, no one was leaving St. Mary's Hospital and I had the school to keep me busy. But George was quite upset about all the changes and although he never was involved in hospital politics, he could see the writing on the wall.

Time flies very fast, and as my grandmother used to say, "The older you get, the faster time flies." I didn't really believe that old saying back then, but now I can see that it really is true.

In the mid-sixty's, George built a beautiful new office in Lewiston, which was very close to the hospital, and now he didn't have to drive his car, he could easily walk there. And if one of his patients had an emergency, George could get to the hospital right away. Our home was very lovely and George loved to cook and he loved entertaining. My job was to decorate the tables and that was all. We had so many beautiful parties, especially at Christmas time.

In the meantime, our boys were growing and getting ready to go to high school. George found out that not too far from our home in Lewiston there was a wonderful educational institution, Hebron Academy, which had an excellent scholastic reputation. Some of our friends' children attended that school. So we decided to send them there too. We sent Georgie there first and then Mark.

The students could "board" at the academy but it was less expensive for them to commute to school and back every day. So, we had to drive them to downtown Lewiston, and there they boarded their bus for Hebron. My boys were very happy there and their classes were very small. And the children had good attention from their teachers. The Academy had all kinds of activities, especially sports, and the boys liked it very much. George and I were happy also because we knew that our sons would receive the very best education.

I was lucky because a few days before we left to go to my meeting in New York, my cousin Doris came from Germany to stay with us for a few months. Now I didn't have to worry about who would stay with my boys and my mother because they had both Mrs. O and Doris.

In October of nineteen eighty-five, George and I left for New York to attend my meeting. On Saturday, suddenly George became very ill with a severe, severe pain in his lower abdomen. I took him to the emergency room of a local New York City hospital and an intern diagnosed him as having acute prostatitis. George was given some pills, and we went back to our hotel.

But George kept getting worse, and I didn't want to keep him in New York. We took a taxi to the airport and by ten P.M. that night, we were back in Lewiston. We went directly to the emergency room at St. Mary's Hospital. I called Dr. M and he came and took x-rays and they diagnosed George as having a ruptured abdominal aneurysm. Can you imagine how upset and frightened I was because that is a very, very serious disease. Then I called Dr. I and other anesthesia staff, and they prepared George for his surgery. When George was ready to go to the operating room, I called Dr. L at home and I told him what was happening to George. He came to the hospital right away and what a wonderful dedicated cardiologist he was. He stayed with George all night just in case he needed a cardiac treatment.

George was very sick after the surgery and had to be on a ventilator for a day or two in the Intensive Care Unit, and they kept him in the hospital for about two weeks. And to my surprise, he recovered very quickly from that terrible illness.

George was then sixty-five and after a couple of months at home, he returned to his office. I advised him that because of his age and sickness, he should no longer deliver babies and that he should only take care of his gynecological surgery and his office patients. George was very reluctant to do this, but after a few months he realized that he could not deliver babies as before.

After a few months of taking care of his maternity patients, he abolished maternity care in his office. Then for another ten years, he only took care of gynecological and office patients. And he also continued to help other surgeons with their operations.

In the meantime, my work was continuing and I was still very, very busy with my anesthesia school and night calls. I forgot to mention that in the late seventies, Margaret left to care for her children. In the late nineteen seventies, we hired Dr. K to a permanent position. He was very conscientious and hard working. Now there were three full-time doctors, along with Dr. Dorothy, who was part time. We also had four nurse anesthetists and several medical students.

I forgot to mention that when Dr. A started to work, he was diagnosed with tuberculosis and he was in a Hebron sanatorium for nearly a year. After having a lobectomy (chest surgery) he recovered very well. And that was a horrible and difficult year for me because, again, I did not have enough help. In the meantime, we got a newcomer to our anesthesia department, Dr. Nancy, she was trained in Detroit and she was excellent and she was ten years younger than me. She worked full time but she didn't stay at St. Mary's very long because her husband, who was a physician, decided to return to Tokyo. So she left with him and they both worked in a hospital there for a while.

Well, it wasn't very long before I received a letter from her wanting me to give her back her job. Unfortunately, I already had enough people and there was no place for her. So I called Dr. M to hire her and he did. Now, all of this was a strange coincidence, to me anyway. Because, at first, I was Dr. Nancy's "chief" at St. Mary's Hospital, and later on, she was my "chief" when I worked with her at Central Maine Medical Center.

Now at St. Mary's, we had enough people to do the work, but it was still difficult to run my school, fill out the papers, and teach the students. Then I hired Barbara, a nurse anesthetist from Waterville. She was a big help because she did all the administrative jobs. Barbara was a very good and dedicated worker and now my job was so much easier.

As I mentioned before, all of our nurses were very smart and dedicated. Please excuse me if I don't mention everyone I worked with, because with that amount of staff and that many years, it's impossible to remember everyone. It wouldn't be fair to one of the girls, Ms. Mailhot, if I didn't praise her too. I knew her from the day she started at St. Mary's and I was always impressed with her work ethic and the way she alone, raised her two children. She later happily married a wonderful doctor and they resided in Lewiston.

From the very beginning, when I was working in Ohio, I belonged to the American Medical Association and the American Medical Anesthesiologist Association. And when I came to Maine, I also belonged to both of these associations in Maine. Once a month, we would have a meeting in different places in Maine and Dr. M, a good friend, would accompany me to the meetings. To my very big surprise, when it came time for the election of new officers, Dr. M nominated me for president! I really couldn't believe it! At first I was shocked and scared but then I thought—*why not! You have another chance to shine!* I was the first to be elected as a woman President in the American Medical Anesthesiology Society of Maine. And I held this position for two years.

Now my boys have finished at the Hebron Academy and they have started college. George finished with a Bachelor's Degree in English and Geography and got a Master's in Environmental and City Planning. Mark had a Bachelor's Degree in International Affairs and he went for a Master's Degree in Business. And then he was accepted at Georgetown

University to study Law and he graduated with a Law Degree. Georgie was very much like his father because he loved living in Maine and upon graduating with a Master's Degree in Environmental Planning from Towson University in Maryland, he returned to live and work in Lewiston.

In the meantime, all of George's family moved from New York. Mary and her husband went to live close to her daughter in Philadelphia. Her son-in-law taught in LaSalle Collage and she taught in a high school in Philadelphia. Paula and her husband left New York and moved outside of Washington and they stayed near Martha, their daughter.

Now I started to realize that people my parents age were starting to die away. I then had some very bad news, Maria's father had died. Very shortly after, it was not even a year, George's brother-in-law died, and then it seemed that somebody we knew was always dying.

One day George came home and told me that it was time for us to retire. That really upset me because I was not ready to retire. With a heavy heart, I thought, I'm still healthy, I'm still strong, I'm not ready to leave my life's work, work that I truly loved. We were looking for a new anesthesiologist who would work with us, and I decided that I would pay him extra to take my night calls.

About ten years before I retired, I assigned the chief position to Dr. A, but he was reluctant because there were many things that he didn't want to do. So I promised that I would help him.

Suddenly, because of misunderstandings with the new anesthesiologist and our new administrator, I finally decided to retire. I packed my books and with a heavy heart and horrible disappointment, I left, without even getting a goodbye party or a word of thanks. After all, I had worked there day and night with deep dedication for nearly forty-two years, and that job was always first and foremost in my mind.

On the very next day after I left St. Mary's Hospital, I found out that they closed the School of Nurse Anesthesia which I had run for twenty-five years. It seems that my colleagues did not want to work as hard in the school as I had.

When I was close to leaving St. Mary's Hospital, my good friend, Dr. Victor, introduced me to Dr. Hector. He was semi-retired and was an orthopedic surgeon in Boston. When his medical work became too much for him, he moved to Maine and went to work at Pineland. Dr. Hector sent patients from Pineland to Dr. Victor and they cared for children and adults with scoliosis.

One day we were talking and I told him that he must have had a very lonely life because there wasn't much work for him at Pineland. He didn't have to worry about night calls, etc. To my surprise, he told me that not only was he a doctor, he was also an artist and that he painted all the time now because he had lots of spare time. He invited me to his home and I nearly fainted; he had hundreds of beautiful, beautiful oil paintings. I couldn't believe how much time he must have spent to do those paintings. We talked about art and I told him that I was still working at the hospital and that I too, love to paint. He asked me why I didn't paint and I told him that I just didn't have the time. He looked at me and said, "For art, you should always find the time." I told him that I didn't know what kind of paint to buy or what paper to use. I told him I didn't know anything about painting.

He told me not to worry and from that day on Hector became my mentor in art, and George was very happy for me. He never minded what I was doing. I was still working, and Hector told me that I must go to school. I couldn't believe it! I really was so ignorant about art. I thought that when you had paper and paints, that's all you needed to become an artist. I didn't know that you had so much to learn to be an artist; after all, it wasn't like studying a foreign language.

Hector started to show me his painting techniques and when he saw what I had done, he said, "Boy, you don't paint, you just smear the paint onto your papers." Then he told me that we were going to take some night classes at Lewiston High School. Some of the classes were with oil paints and others were with water colors, and I found the classes to be very difficult. But I continued because I really love art.

I was working at Central Maine Medical Center and I didn't have night calls any longer so I was able to study art and paint more. Then Hector told me that if I really wanted to become a good artist, we should take some art classes at the University of Maine. That was a big shock to me because I now considered myself to be an "old" woman.

Hector persuaded me to accompany him to the painting classes at the university. Now you wouldn't believe it. I loved it! I took all kinds of night classes and I really was a full-time student. It was very hard for me, but to my surprise, I loved it. The students were about my own children's ages and they were very kind to me. They never once laughed at me or made me feel that I was an old grandma. I really enjoyed going to my classes at the University of Maine and I think I learned so very much from Hector's art expertise, and to this very day, I am deeply appreciative of Hector's friendship.

When I finally finished all my classes, I was nearly eighty; it hadn't cost me any money because I was a "senior citizen." I wanted to get a Bachelor's Degree in Fine Art. When I told the Dean of Admissions what I wanted, she told me that in order to have a Bachelor's Degree from the University of Maine, I must show them my degrees in English, history and math. I already had my M.D. and a Ph.D., but that didn't seem to impress them at all.

Well, when I finished all of my art classes and I had sadness in my heart because I felt that after attending those classes, I deserved to have a Bachelor's Degree in Fine Art. But all the time, even until today, if I have the chance, I still take an art class. Because in art, you never finish learning, and even until this very day, whenever we have a chance, Dr. Hector and I still paint together.

Then my very good friend Dr. Richard, who at that time was Chief of the Anesthesia Department at Central Maine Medical Center, asked me to work for them, and I accepted. But George was not very happy because he had completely retired. I worked there for three years and I had a wonderful time and they treated me like a queen. I didn't have to take night calls; I only worked from eight until four. I mostly did pre-ops and replaced people when they took their breaks. I received excellent pay, better than St. Mary's. In nineteen ninety-seven, when I retired from the Central Maine Medical Center, they gave me a lovely retirement party.

On August first, nineteen eighty-nine, our oldest son Georgie and Cheryl decided to get married and they had a beautiful wedding. All of our family came to Lewiston for the ceremony, and my future daughter-in-law, Cheryl, wanted the ceremony to be held in the Holy Cross Church where she was baptized. Their beautiful wedding reception was held at

Lost Valley where our family had spent so many happy years doing the skiing that they loved so much.

Then Mark became engaged and they decided to get married on May sixth, two thousand. Because our fiftieth anniversary was on October twenty-first, he wanted us to move our anniversary to his wedding day so that we could celebrate together.

Upon retiring, George had placed his medical office for sale, but nobody wanted to buy it so he gave it to our son Mark who turned into his private rental office. Later on, Mark paid us for the office building.

During the first few years of our retirement, we would go to George's niece, Martha, in Washington to join his relatives in a family Christmas. Then we would go to Florida and stay about six weeks. We needed return to Maine at the end of March to do our income taxes, and it was now getting very hot in Florida and we didn't like it.

George's sister, Ivanka, married for the second time, and they moved from Toronto to Florida for the winter. They purchased a small house next to the Ukrainian community in Northport and they wanted us to stay next to them in the winter. To my surprise, I found a huge Ukrainian community with a brand new beautiful Ukrainian Catholic Church with a smaller Orthodox Church and a large settlement of condominiums mostly for Ukrainians.

We had a chance to purchase a very small condominium in Venice, Florida on the ocean. It was in a beautiful park within walking distance to the ocean. The price was very reasonable so we purchased the condo and spent many happy days there before my George passed. To our surprise, Doris' daughter, Oksana, and her family came for a visit. She was a teacher and he was an atomic-energy engineer and they lived in France. They had two boys and they stayed about two weeks. I was very pleased and so happy to see her.

Ivanka insisted that on Sundays we had to go to the Ukrainian Catholic Church in Northport. One Sunday, when I saw the priest who celebrated the mass, he seemed very familiar to me. He was tall and very good looking but I could not place him. I asked Ivanka his name and she told me, he was Father Woloszczuk. Upon hearing his name, I vividly remembered who he was. When we were in training in Ohio, many years ago, he was a student of theology. He was married to a lovely young lady and they had a few children. We were very friendly with them. But after leaving Ohio in nineteen fifty-five, we never heard about their family again.

After all those years, people change and after mass, we were reintroduced and we were invited to their hospitable home. Their home was beautiful in a very special section of town. Father Woloszczuk told us his long story. Upon graduation, the Ukrainian priests in America were doing very poorly financially, and he was afraid that he wouldn't be able to support his wife and three children. So he went to work in Akron, Ohio until his children graduated from school and then he enrolled in the priesthood. He held services in Ohio for all Ukrainian people. Then he moved to Florida and he became a permanent parish priest in Northport.

After spending a few winters in Florida, George told me that he didn't want anything more to do with our condominium and that he had decided to give it to Mark, but we would continue paying the upkeep and taxes. Mark was so happy to have that home and he made it very beautiful. Even though we would always go to Florida, I didn't really like it there and I was always happy to return to our home in Maine.

I could see that my George wasn't feeling that well. He was never depressed and he was always a happy-go-lucky man. I couldn't really tell if he was unwell or just hated being retired. He was beginning to gain weight, so he started to take long walks along the beach. Then he began losing weight, and I was very worried about him all the time. George went for medical tests and everything was fine and we had a beautiful time in Florida.

Then on the twenty-fifth of March, Paula, George's sister who lived in Washington, came for a visit and she stayed with us. George really didn't feel like cooking dinner for all of us but he did it anyway.

On Friday morning around eight o'clock, George was still in bed and I heard him call out for me. He said that he was very sick with a sharp pain between his shoulders. I went to the bathroom to get him some medicine and when I came back, he was unconscious; he had no pulse and he was not breathing. I resuscitated him and when he regained consciousness, he said that he was feeling a little better. His blood pressure was somewhat low and I called nine-one-one and the ambulance took him to the Sarasota Memorial Hospital. I felt hopeful about him going there because this hospital is rated one of the ten best hospitals in the United States.

At the hospital George underwent emergency abdominal surgery, and the doctors found that he was suffering from a thoracic dissecting aneurysm, which was a very serious condition. I was in a total state of shock. I didn't know what to do; all I could do was to pray and pray. *Please Good Lord, don't let my George die. Please, please God, please save him.* I couldn't think what my life would be like without George and I never really thought that I might lose him. I called our good friend, Father Woloszczuk, and he came right away and he supported me.

George's surgery lasted about eight hours and he was given five units of blood. But God didn't hear my prayers after all because when the doctor came out of surgery, he told me that my George was still alive but he was in very serious condition. So immediately I called both Mark and Georgie and they flew down to Florida the following day, which was Saturday, but George went into kidney failure and paralysis from the waist down. He died at five a.m. on Sunday morning. The date was March twenty-six, two thousand. My darling George was only eighty years old.

Thank God for our two sons because they knew just what to do to help both me and their father. We had a beautiful service in the funeral home in Florida. We arranged the ceremony for George, and the funeral home was packed with people. Because he was so well-known, several priests, and many of our friends, and others too numerous to mention, all came to pay their last respects to my George.

We brought George back to Boundbrook, New Jersey by plane and we buried him in the Ukrainian Cemetery where so many of our relatives are buried.

After George's funeral, I returned to Lewiston and then my poor dog, BiBi, died about a week after George. My house was so very empty; I didn't want to live there alone. I had nocturnal phobia, which I got from my mother. I was so scared and so alone that I would stay up all night watching television. When morning came, I would go upstairs to sleep in the daytime. After George's death, Mark asked me to go stay with him in Washington. I stayed about two weeks and then I came home to stay with Georgie for about one week. Because I felt much better in my own home, I returned to my home in Lewiston.

But with George gone, I was so alone and now the horrible time is starting. All those "so called friends" who had shared George's and my life, now became indifferent to me. Thank God that I still had our relatives and Maria and Olesia. They couldn't help me much but at least they tried. I was so lost without my George. I told myself that I had to pull myself together and I have to work, work, work.

Then Olesia, my cousin who was also alone and a brilliant interior decorator, came to stay with me. I was not an architect but I decided that I was going to build myself a new, beautiful house on Taylor Pond where our old camp was located. I called a builder and he came to look at the plans I had drawn up. He had to go to the city planning board and they would not allow us to build it because it was against their rules because it was on a pond. So I hired a third man, and along with my son George, who has a Masters Degree in Environmental Planning, we took our plans to the city council and we finally got them approved, but they were much changed.

With Olesia's help, we started to build our house. It took from two thousand until two thousand and one, a whole year. I think that if it wasn't for her, I would never have had such a beautiful interior to my home. Then I gave our other home in Lewiston to George and his wife. I was so happy that my George had gotten to see his first granddaughter, Larissa, who was born in nineteen ninety-nine, before he passed away.

Then autumn came and Olesia came to stay with me because I didn't want to stay alone in Florida. The same year that Olesia helped me to build my house, Georgie and his wife went to Bar Harbor on vacation. But Olesia and I went to Souzivka, in New York, to Ukrainian gatherings.

When we returned, I heard by phone that my son Georgie was very sick and was in the hospital. I went to see him, and Georgie had a horrible disease called acute fulminating pancreatitis. He was hospitalized for three whole months. He had about eight different doctors and they didn't know how to treat him. We finally found Dr. I, and she operated and removed his diseased gallbladder. Georgie recovered very well and he soon returned to work.

Because of his father's death, Mark wanted to postpone his wedding. But I insisted that he go ahead because his wedding plans were all arranged. I put on a good face but my heart was very sad because my George wasn't there. It just goes to show you that if you have an anniversary, never postpone it because we, George and I, should have celebrated our fiftieth wedding anniversary on October twenty-first and not wait to celebrate it with Mark.

The wedding was very beautiful, but nobody wanted to dance. Two priests, one of whom was our dear friend, Father Paschak, and all of George's and my family came to Mark's wedding party. Mark made his home in Clifton, Virginia and opened his law firm with his wife Vicki and several other lawyers. About a year later, I had some very good news; Mark told me that they had had a baby girl and they had named her Caroline. Now I have two beautiful granddaughters, Larissa, who is fourteen and Caroline, who is twelve.

Summers, I stayed in Lewiston but in the fall I would go to my Florida apartment, and Olesia would come with me. I met a wonderful artist, Carolyn, there, who was also an art teacher, and she assembled meetings for artists who were willing to paint with her. I joined the Ukrainian Catholic Church and I met so many people and many of my old friends there. At that time there was a large Ukrainian community and parishes of Ukrainian Catholic and Orthodox parishioners with all kinds of activities.

* * * * *

I never liked to cook and when we came to Maine I tried to find any free moment to take George to eat at a restaurant. Someone told us that in Auburn there was a very good restaurant and we should go there. They served mostly a "chicken" menu and we went a few times. One day we went and to my surprise there was sign that said, "Rolandeau"s Restaurant." I was introduced to a new and very young owner and his mother who had bought the restaurant. He was the owner and chef, and his mother was the dessert specialist. They had a very French atmosphere, and to my taste, the food was excellent; and because they specialized in lobster and seafood dishes, they were always very busy. And what a coincidence, the young owner's mother was an excellent skater, and because my husband George was crazy about hockey, they had much in common. This lady owned a skating school and George wanted the boys to play hockey as soon they could and to play. George enrolled both our boys in her Sunday hockey classes.

When we opened the recovery room, we hired another nurse, Mrs. Figorlie, who was an excellent, excellent nurse. I remember vividly that she would have her daughter visit her with her two grandchildren. One of them was a boy named Nicki and he was about eight years old. Would you believe it, after he grew up, he joined Rolandeau's Restaurant and he is still there today. He is an excellent bartender and his other passion is that he loves horses. I will always appreciate the Rolandeau's Restaurant staff for their services and kindness to both me and George.

New Husband:

After George's passing, I was very lonely and I felt very alone. That winter, I returned to Florida with my cousin Olesia and live in my apartment that I later gave to my son Mark. And I still felt very, very alone. Quite by accident, once again, I met Bohdan Wysocky, a man who had been my brother, Myron's, best friend. They had gone to school together, and Bohdan had been with my brother when he died. I had known Bohdan when he was a young man of seventeen.

As I became reacquainted with Bohdan, and as he told me stories of his time spent with my brother Myron, I began to feel very close to him and he seemed like my brother. Bohdan had been a widower for eight years, and we started going out together. Finally we decided to get married so that we could live together and help and support each other in our old age.

Bohdan preferred to live in Florida and since his house was really too small for both of us, we decided to build a new home to our liking. And with his plans, the house turned out beautiful. We still live in Florida in our new home during the long Maine winters.

In Conclusion:

I decided to write my book, not "to be famous or to become a writer," but I wrote my story for my children, George and Mark Dycio, and their families. Now I have a few words for my grandchildren, my great-grandchildren, for my other relatives, and my very good friends.

I want them to see what a hard life—not just me—but my relatives, and friends have had. And to tell you once again that never, never should we have another war. War brings no luck to anyone. War only brings misery, horror, and death to so many. It brings misery and death to old people, and poor young men and women who return from battle without legs, or are blind, without faces—for what good? In a few years, another war and we will have the same results. I know that they had to fight Hitler and Stalin. They were the worst devils known to mankind, and the misery they created was beyond description. I want to tell my readers, that you don't really understand the horrors of war until you have lived through it.

To My Grandchildren:

You should know and remember that you who live in these United States are born with "silver spoons" in your mouths. Why do I say this? Because I can tell you, I have been practically all over the world and there is nowhere, nowhere in the whole wide world, which is such a good place as the United States of America. Not only do you have freedom, but you have a million or more opportunities to do whatever you wish with your life. If somebody is lazy and doesn't want to work, well, that's just too bad. But if you are young and you are healthy and you are motivated, there isn't anything you can't do. You should give thanks morning, noon and night that you have been born in these United States. Because, in my opinion, the United States is the best place in the whole wide world. It is a "God given country" and it the land of milk and honey. You should get down on your knees both morning and night and thank the Good Lord that you were chosen to live here. I can tell you here and now that my happiest day was not when I got married, not when I got my diploma in medicine either. Not when my sons were born—it was when I got my American citizenship. Because you don't know what it means to be without a country. When you have no country to call your own, you float in the air and you don't know who wants to kill you or to send you back to another unwanted place. You just float in the air and you have no rights. You can't imagine how very lucky my George and I and my parents were to become American citizens. We all cried with happiness, and I hope my children, my grandchildren, my great-grandchildren, my relatives and my friends all understand what I am trying to say, and that is . . .

May God bless the United States of America and may God bless my husband Bohdan, my children, my grandchildren, all of my family, my friends and my ghostwriter and scribe, Martha Stevens-David, too. And Sultan, my beautiful dog, I love him so much.

Final Words and Acknowledgements

Finally, one last word to all my good friends, who are still alive. I want to wish them much success and good health. Especially to my good friends like Dr. and Mrs. Richard Marshall, Dr. and Mrs. Cyprian Martel and Dr. Cloutier, who were so very good to me. Poor Dr. Fishman, he died about three years after George. I miss Dr. Fishman very much and Mrs. Fishman, who has always been wonderful to me and who still resides in Auburn, Maine. I also miss poor Dr. Morin, who died three months before my George and I am still in touch with my dear friend, Mrs. Morin.

So many of our good friends have now died, and it is so difficult to understand how your friends can die. I would like to wish all of my remaining friends, good health and good luck. I should also like to mention the two Dr. Reeves who died after George passed away because they were always so caring about me.

It wouldn't be fair not to mention my cousin Orest, because he is my father's beloved sister's son. By the end of the Communists occupation, they came to his wife's family in Toronto, Canada. Their two sons remained in Ukraine to study computers and medicine, and after they completed their studies, they came to Canada. I truly admire his younger son, and through a very big hardship, he and his wife finished their training in the United States. Now they reside in New York and both work there as anesthesiologists. The reason I mention them is that

I admire their perseverance because I know how very hard they worked because I went through this also.

One last thing I wanted to mention. I am now an artist. I paint and I love to draw and I drew a beautiful monument for our grave. It is made of dark granite and is engraved with both George's and my names. Because, when I die I will be buried next to my darling George.

And I just want to tell you how lucky I am to be ninety-one years old. I can still drive my car, still see well enough to paint when I want and I can still use my brain and take good care of myself. I truly feel that the "Powers that Be" have been very good to me. All of my life, I have been very religious and I don't know what my life would have been like if I did not believe in the Good Lord. He was the one who always gave me strength, hope and a little bit of sunshine.

Maria Myroslava "Gloria" Tanczak –Dycio, September 5, 2013

**My Medical
School Document**

George Dycio

George and My Wedding

George and My Wedding

George Dycio's Parents

George, Me and My Parents

My Parents

My Parents, George and Me

Me and Our First Chevrolet

My Parents in the United States

Our Family Reunion - 1952

Me & BiBi

Me - 1952
Anesthesia Residency
Canton, Ohio

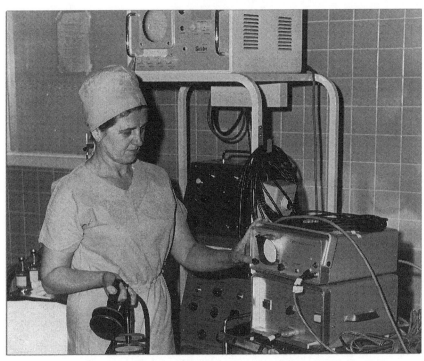

Me with Anesthesia Machine at St. Mary's Hospital

A Family Gathering

Mrs. Ouelette, George, Me and Cousin

George, Me and Sons

Dr. George Dycio - Marine Reserves

Me - St. Mary's Hospital

**Sons -
Georgie
and Mark**

Mark and Georgie Dycio

Family Reunion - 1963

Family Gathering

Me and Sons

Dr. George Dycio and Sons

The Dycio Family

Georgie and Mark Dycio

Our Boat on Taylor Pond, Auburn, ME

1970
MEDICAL STAFF OF ST. MARY'S GENERAL HOSPITAL

Father's Ukrainian Church - New Brunswick, NJ

Dr. George Dycio - St. Mary's Hospital

Me - St. Mary's Hospital

George and Nieces

Dycio Family

George and Me in Puerto Rico

Me - St. Mary's Hospital

George and Cheryl Dycio's Wedding

Mark and Vicki Dycio's Wedding

Mark's Wedding - George, Me and Mark

Mark and Vicki Dycio's Wedding

Larissa and Carolyne - Granddaughters

Sons - George and Mark Dycio

Me and Bohdan Wysocki - Marriage

My 90th Birthday

My Parents' Burial Place
St. Peter's Cemetery, Boundbrook, NJ

George and My Burial Plot
St. Andrews Ukrainian Cemetery, Boundbrook, NJ

My Dog, Sultan

About the Author

In July of 2012, I was approached to scribe the autobiography of the very well-known Dr. Mary Tanczak-Dycio. I immediately recognized that this recording of her ninety-plus years would be life changing for both of us. And I was not disappointed. We agreed to meet at her beautiful home in Auburn, Maine, and thus began our nearly two-year journey trying to capture the very essence of her long and productive life. From the tales of her birth in 1922, in West Ukraine, through to her present day life, I was constantly reminded that I was in the presence of a very accomplished lady. Not only has Dr. Dycio mastered our American English, she is proficient in seven other languages as well.

Even as a small child, Dr. Dycio was enthralled with the idea of being a doctor and she never let go of her dream. With great courage, determination and focus, she followed her medical dream. from a tiny Ukrainian village in the throes of World War Two, across many international borders from one war-torn country to another, until she finally landed on the shores of the United States of America in 1950 where she became a board certified doctor and specialist in Anesthesiology. She and her Ukrainian husband, George, an Ob-Gyn, settled in Maine in 1957 where they continued their medical professions until they retired, and raised two sons.

In 2013, Dr. Mary, as she is so affectionately called by all who have the privilege of knowing her, is entering her twilight years with the same tenacity and kindness for others that has been her calling card throughout her long life. And I say, 'May God bless and keep you, Mary, because I know, you will not go softly into your good night'.

Martha Stevens-David

Chronology of Aging

I'm young, she said as she danced by
Graceful as a butterfly
And young she was the truth be told
For she was only six years old...

I'm young, she said to one and all
As she danced her prom dress down the hall
And young she was the truth be known
The sixteen years had really flown...

I'm young, she said at thirty-three
And what the years have done to me
The birth of babies, one and two
One with brown eyes, one with blue...

I'm young, she said but not so sure
As she softly closed the kitchen door
I'm forty-five and still quite thin
It just depends what clothes I'm in...

I'm still quite young, she keeps repeating
But I've got to learn to control my eating
Fifty-five, it's not too bad
I wonder why I feel so sad...

I'm not that old, she often thinks
As she washes dishes at the sink
It's not so old this sixty-three
As she dances grandchildren on her knee...

I once was young, she said with grace
As she smoothes the wrinkles on her face
The years have flown I know not where
And ask me if I really care...

She seemed so young, they all said
As they fluffed the pillows at her head
Tears fell down as they filed past
This look at her would be their last...

An original poem by Martha Stevens-David© 2009

Made in the USA
Middletown, DE
02 June 2017